Inside the Colleges of Further Education

Adrian Bristow

London
Her Majesty's Stationery Office

A

ISBN 0 11 270331 3

Contents

A little of the material in Chapters 1, 6 and 10 appeared in a different form in *Technical Education and Industrial Training* and is reprinted with the permission of the publishers.

The publishers would like to express their thanks to the GLC for permission to reproduce a copyright illustration and to the *Radio Times, Hulton Picture Library*.

A word in your ear . . .

This is an attempt to write a cheerful and engaging account of life and work in a college of further education. I have set out to explode the myths, unveil the mysteries, and reveal the college of further education in its new true image to the interested parent and the intelligent layman.

To write a readable book about colleges of further education is a formidable task which one could only undertake lightly. I have done my best but I must warn you, gentle reader, that if you are looking for the definitive textbook on technical education, illumined by scholarship and refined by research, then I am afraid you have bought the wrong book. Neither is this book meant for my colleagues in the colleges though it may cause them a certain amount of innocent merriment. I hope, however, that, since education is a unity, this book may be of some interest and value to colleagues in the schools—particularly careers teachers, headteachers and others who advise pupils on their futures.

This book is called *Inside the Colleges of Further Education* but it could well have been called 'Inside the Technical Colleges' because the two are the same.

This name, College of Further Education, which we have grown used to hearing during the last few years, was introduced in 1944. It is meant to emphasise that education is a continuing process and that after the primary and secondary stages comes a further stage for those who have left school. A college of further education does the same work as a technical college and I shall use the titles quite indiscriminately to give variety.

I shall also use the terms further education and technical education equally indiscriminately. I know that further education embraces technical education and a good deal else but it seems pointless to make a distinction which exists only for the purist—which you and I are not. Further education (or FE) is what we call the multifarious activities of a technical college or a college of further education. I shall use it in this sense and I shall also use it to mean the colleges themselves as in 'we in FE', for example. It helps to relieve tedious repetition.

Technical education is a complex and confusing subject and difficult to reduce to simple terms for those who have only had experience of primary and secondary schools. I have sought to convey something of the essence of life in a college of FE and something of the activities of the thousands of students of all ages, abilities, and backgrounds. I have also tried to give, without seeming to do so, as much useful information as I felt the layman could comfortably stomach.

My little book deals with your local college. This may be a small one or a large one but it is the college to which your son or daughter could go for further education.

I must confess I have no personal experience of the very large college mainly engaged in what we call 'advanced' work, that is work above GCE A level or for which A level qualifications are a condition of entry. (Remember this definition if you can—it's important.)

I am a local college man. I have been principal of a small local college and I now manage a biggish one where the natural ceiling is A level or its equivalent. It is in these run-of-the-mill colleges where the bulk of further education is carried on. We are the bedrock of further education—not, I hasten to add, the rockbottom.

I was surprised and delighted to be asked by the Department of Education and Science (let's call it DES for short in future) to write this book. No one had ever invited me to write anything before and, as Wilde said, 'Nothing annoys people more than not receiving invitations'.

A.J.B.
Chester 1976

CHAPTER ONE

Fact and fantasy

*It was touching to see these three big men, with the marks
of their hard labour about them, anxiously bending over
the worn books, and painfully making out,
'The grass is green', 'The sticks are dry', 'The corn is ripe'.
It was almost as if three rough animals were making
humble efforts to learn how they might become human.*

Adam Bede George Eliot

Grey clouds hang low over the sodden moors. Down in the
valley, smoke from a dozen tall chimneys climbs Lowry-like
out of the gloom to meet and mingle with the lowering sky.

There are small towns down there, crouching under the
lee of the hills. Clogs ring on the dank cobbles and through
the drizzle sad figures in cloth-caps and shawls pass to and
fro.

It is early evening. There is a smell of cowheel on the air
and somewhere a male voice choir is calling. In a side-street
near the market stands a forbidding red-brick building,
streaked with the grime of generations. The windows are tall
and set high up in the walls. Gas jets flare through the
grubby panes and inside shaggy-haired apprentices sprawl
over their desks. They are laboriously copying down notes
which the instructor has just laboriously written up on the
blackboard. The process of technical education is being
carried on.

This is the image that 'technical college' still conjures up
for too many people. It is at its most potent among those
who believe that the north of England starts just outside
Heal's in the Tottenham Court Road. We see instruction (as
opposed to teaching) in craft subjects being given at night in
depressing premises by part-time unqualified staff to apprentices of limited ability from humble backgrounds. All
the unlovely elements of our historical origin are here, that
origin which, until a few years ago, we carried like some
educational albatross around our neck.

1

Technical education emerged from the squalor of the industrial revolution. Technical institutions were built in the heart of the towns they served and became identified with the dirt and muck around them. This picture holds all the folk-memory of technical education.

This is our 'night school' image. Night school! The term is as emotive as 'workhouse master' or 'labouring poor'. So apt, so enduring, it haunts us even now and mocks our aspirations. It still smacks of the superior artisan striving to better himself on the frail foundation of an inadequate elementary education. This is how we have been seen until recently by a large and influential section of the public.

There is another view of FE, more sinister perhaps in its implications because it is held by some inside the teaching profession—and others outside it. This is based upon a mixture of observation, hearsay, envy, and prejudice, and is concerned more with present appearances than with historical origins. It is derived from such a scene as this.

Slyme Green College of FE lies to the north of the town on the edge of a vast new trading estate. A glistening block of glass and concrete, it was opened a little over two years ago by Councillor Haddock, Mayor of Slyme Green and Chairman of Governors. A trail of litter leads you up the drive, past the savaged saplings to the pool in the forecourt, a feature full of orange peel, cigarette packs and little bits of stick. In the middle on a slab of slate stands a thing in metal symbolising the birth of technical education.

The actual entrance consists of a baffling number of glass doors, some locked, some boarded up. Starting from the left you try the handles in turn and finally find yourself in a grubby foyer.

A sign says 'All visitors must report to the college office'. But the enquiries hatch is shut and there is no sign of life. Opposite the office are two lifts, one marked 'Out of Order', the other 'Not to be used by students'. Slumped on the stairs, an unshaven caretaker puffs unsteadily away in an aroma of brown ale.

Suddenly a nerve-shattering clangour. No, it isn't a fire, it's break. There is a Gadarene rush for refreshment by staff

Further education now—and then. In place of the old buildings stand 'glittering blocks of glass and concrete'.

Lunch-time alternatives: time for a chat with friends in the college's pleasant grounds or for a tasty snack in the refectory.

The college office is a key information point for students and the public.

A quiet place to study and to 'make new discoveries and extend horizons'.

The range of the work has widened enormously since the early days of night-schools (above). Technical and engineering courses reflect industrial advances.

and students with the latter lying a bad second. Down the battered corridors to the refectory charges the young idea to drink dark tea slopped into chipped cups. Here the floor is a mess of bottles and cigarette packets and the tables are piled high with dirty crockery. Feet up on the broken chairs, apprentices linger round the vending machine in a sea of cardboard cups. One lad is steadily feeding the machine with washers he has just made in the workshop.

The students' common room is filled with smoke and the whole place is vibrating so much to Rod Stewart's latest that you can hardly hear the cry of 'Pay pontoons and five cards only'.

But in the lavatories all is still, the silence broken only by the scratching of biros on scarred walls. This is graffitti time. Kilroy has been here and he seems to have taken most of the fittings with him.

That shattering bell again. Break is officially over. The staff settle down to a second cup of tea and a figure in an old raincoat pedals up the drive and puts his bicycle in the section reserved for kitchen staff. The caretaker teeters confidingly forward. 'Ere's the principal now, mate.'

Exaggerated? Distorted? Well, yes. But this disagreeable little sketch does contain several of the elements which, though grossly inflated, conjure up the college of FE for some teachers in the secondary schools.

They see their local college staffed by untrained men and women with, to them, unheard of and outlandish qualifications of dubious value, engaged upon vocational work of an elementary nature. Forgetting that nearly all the students, apart from a few refugees from the grammar schools and a handful of dissidents from the private sector, come from the schools they themselves teach in, they dismiss the student body as one with little discipline and a sad lack of academic standards. Headteachers see scant concern for such sacred cows as *esprit de corps*, pastoral care, extra-curricular activities and a nice regard for dress.

Yet, despite this, when they contemplate our colleges, see the vast blocks wreathed in technological mystery shouldering their way into the sky, our secondary colleagues admit to a reluctant admiration. Many have little idea what goes on inside (nor do they wish to have really) but they are impressed by the sheer scope of it all. They remain suspicious, however, of some of our advanced work. Inspired by a genuine if misguided fear of debasing the academic coinage, they view with a certain distrust our proliferation of certificates and diplomas in the oddest subjects. Many of those on the arts side, of course, have a natural antipathy—in some cases a shuddering revulsion almost—towards anything that smacks of engineering, science or technology.

Happily, the ordinary public shares neither of these views. Their image of the technical colleges is a very much happier one. To them the 'tech', as they call it, is something clear-cut, real, understandable, acceptable. This is their kind of institution. Sons, brothers and husbands have been going to night-school at the tech for generations. More recently, their sons have been attending day-release classes and their daughters have been taking full-time business studies courses. Millions have direct experience of the technical college, accepting it as part of the natural order of things.

The public's view of the tech is one rooted in reality. The old saying, derived from hard times—'learn a trade and you will never be without a job'—is still current, and has added force when unemployment rises. Applied mathematics, applied science, engineering drawing, workshop practice—this is the very stuff of industrial life. It has a direct bearing on your job in the drawing office or in the machine shop. Theory is related to practice; you learn 'how' at work, the tech teaches you 'why'.* Through the tech you obtain the qualifications which will help you to gain promotion from the workshop floor. This instinctive understanding and appreciation of technical education contrasts sharply and sadly with the attitude of some educationists and many in the teaching profession.

Here then is a great fund of goodwill towards the techs. Let me give you an example. Thousands of men today in managerial and supervisory posts in engineering owe their

---

* In several engineering shops in the United States I saw the slogan, 'The man who knows "how" works for the man who knows "why".'

positions not only to their skill and efforts, but to qualifications gained through part-time study at the tech. This part-time route was the only way open for the aspiring engineer; it was the key to advancement inside the industry and to social mobility outside. And they are proud of having gained their Ordinary National Certificate (ONC) and Higher National Certificate (HNC) the hard way. Most of them, brought up between the wars, had to leave school at fourteen with only an elementary education. In many cases their parents could not afford to send them to a grammar school, for years the poor bright boy's path to advancement. Their only chance to continue their studies and get on was 'night school', attending classes at the local evening institute or at the tech after a day's work.

Three or four nights a week, year after year, they slogged away at maths, science and drawing, slowly hauling themselves rung by rung up the ladder of the National Certificate scheme and beyond. Those who eventually succeeded brought to the industry an integrity plus a blend of craft skill and applied knowledge which is part of an engineering tradition reaching back to Telford, Brindley, and the eighteenth century.

Although this part-time evening route in engineering is virtually closed, the men who followed it remain and they remember with gratitude the work of the pre-war teachers in the techs.

So what is the reality today? What is the truth about the colleges? How much of our historical image actually remains? How accurate is this picture we apparently present to some of our colleagues in the schools? Forward, the iconoclast! Let me shatter the historical image with one stroke of the pen.

Most of the old buildings have been swept away and in their place stand glittering blocks of glass and concrete, bright monuments to the fantastic post-war expansion of further education. It is like the transformation scene in 'Cinderella'. One moment we are in Baron Stoneybroke's kitchen; the next, up flies the gauze, and we stand open-mouthed in the ballroom of the palace. In your town the college of FE is probably one of the most modern and imposing of your civic buildings. Surrounded by trim lawns, and with the best car-parking in town, it is a source of pride (at least, I hope it is) to the local ratepayers.

The outside is more than matched by the quality of the interior. Our modern colleges have superbly equipped workshops, laboratories, lecture theatres, studios and specialist accommodation. The public areas such as foyers, libraries, halls and refectories and lounges are attractively designed, light and spacious, and finished and furnished to a standard that brings admiring glances from visitors.

Because of the rapid growth of further education, some of our original buildings have had to remain in service as annexes. In due course they will be pulled down and the sites redeveloped, but I cannot let them slip into oblivion without a salute, some mark of respect and affection.

I know it is fashionable for many of us in technical education to smile at the tiled walls, echoing lavatories, and flatulent heating systems of these Victorian and Edwardian piles. But they are solid structures, standing four-square, cool in summer and warm and inviting in winter, built of best Accrington brick. So hard are the bricks and so strong is the bond, that you can bore and tunnel and engineer to your heart's content without the building falling down around your ears. Purpose built, they have stood up nobly to what generations of industrial youth chose to inflict upon them.

I am very fond of some of these old institutions, especially the grim giants of the north-west. I hope that one or two of them will be maintained and cherished as mute reminders of part of our educational heritage. But we must be quick or they will be lost to us for ever.

I have in mind the original Warrington Technical College in Palmyra Square built in 1899. This has a most imposing first floor with joinery on the grand scale and an impressive mosaic floor which simply cries out loud for preservation. The old Wigan and District Mining and Technical Institute built in 1896 in Library Street and distinguished for its terracotta work is another such. In buildings like these all over the north, the very heartland of technical education, you can feel the pride of the early pioneers, those generous industrialists, far-sighted councillors, and splendid benefactors. *Si monumentum requiris . . .*

And what about the present? It is not only the buildings that have changed. As I shall demonstrate in later chapters, staff, students and the work itself have radically altered too.

Staff are well-qualified technically and professionally and a large and increasing percentage has had teacher-training.

As for our students, no longer are they working lads taking evening classes in engineering. Now boys and girls from every sort of educational and social background are swelling the numbers in our full-time and sandwich courses. Today there is a vast range of full- and part-time courses at all levels and every chance for the able student to proceed to a degree course or its equivalent. And no longer are our courses simply vocational; colleges are very much involved in general education in a variety of ways.

Lastly, in most areas of our work, 'night school' is virtually dead. Thanks to the rapid growth of day-release, especially in the engineering industry, it was possible to abolish the old pattern of vocational evening classes. To be fair, this does not apply to business studies—or commerce as it used to be called. This spoils my tidy picture, because far too much business education, from shorthand and type-writing to management, is still carried on through the medium of evening classes.

If I claim that the reality is quite different from the myth you may well ask how this sea-change came about. The simple answer is through the vast post-war expansion of technical colleges and their work. Not only has our part-time day-release work grown enormously but, more significantly, there has been this startling development of full-time courses.

In the past, technical colleges were essentially colleges catering for the part-time student. There were few full-time courses and these were mainly restricted to junior commercial courses. However, as the demand for vocational education mounted after the war, Ordinary National and Higher National Diploma courses blossomed, together with a range of full-time courses in such different fields as engineering, business, nursing, hairdressing, catering and building.

As the number of students in full- and part-time courses rose dramatically, there was a vast investment in further education during the 'fifties and early 'sixties in terms of buildings and staff. This spectacular expansion went largely unrecognised by the public, but during these golden years the colleges opened up career opportunities at all levels in many trades and professions. This is the great post-war achievement of further education.

Eventually, however, what the colleges had achieved and were now offering began to seep through into the public consciousness. The process was helped by the increasing stress put by governments of the day upon the vital part technical education had to play in economic expansion.

We used to joke, and still do, about constant references to 'technically-orientated society', 'technological expansion', and so forth. Fortunately they were made so often that some of our magic began to rub off upon a rather reluctant public. With political emphasis and a growing public awareness of our importance came a status and a future undreamed of years before.

Then in the last decade has come the accolade of social acceptance. Unlike Byron, we awoke one morning and found ourselves respectable. Our new full-time courses attracted students, particularly girls, from a wide social background. As we shall see, going to college became very much the thing to do. We had arrived!

You may feel I am a little too concerned about the image the college presents, but it is vitally important for us in FE. For too long our work and reputation have been clouded by the curious ideas I have described. Our present reputation and our future as developing educational institutions depend upon the esteem in which we and our work are held by the public. Although influenced by externals like buildings and equipment, the view the public takes of us ultimately rests upon the quality and relevance of our teaching and on our standards, academic and social. This is how we are judged. And the FE image is the local college!

CHAPTER TWO

Names, aims and claims

What's in a name? that which we call a rose
By any other name would smell as sweet.

Romeo and Juliet William Shakespeare

If you live in a large town it will almost certainly possess a technical college or a college of further education. If you live in a very large town then you may be blessed with a college of technology or, even better, a college of technology and design or, better still, an institute of technology. Do not despair: all these are variations on the basic technical college theme, though they do little to reduce the confusion among the public.

I must admit I like the proud simple ring of 'technical college' even though our local colleges are increasingly being called colleges of FE. This seems reasonable enough since the concept and title, further education, has become widely accepted during the last decade. If the technical college travels under various aliases, the 600-plus colleges together do form a national structure, a bit ramshackle but a structure nevertheless. This is like a pyramid but it is by no means a uniform one. Nothing in FE is ever uniform!

At the base of the pyramid are the local colleges of FE, usually serving a well-defined community. These can be large institutions and many today commonly have well over one hundred full-time members of staff. The normal ceiling of their work is Ordinary National Certificate (ONC) or Diploma (OND), the final stages of craft and technician courses, and GCE A level.

The next layer in the pyramid consists of colleges which may serve a city or draw their students from a large rural area with several towns. These colleges normally cover the same work as the local colleges but also run some specialised and advanced courses such as Higher National Certificate (HNC) and Diploma (HND). I should stress that these are not hard and fast distinctions and the lines between local and area colleges are becoming blurred; even local colleges may do advanced work within very narrow limits.

At the top of the pyramid are the regional colleges, major institutions which again cover much of the work done by local and area colleges but in addition carry out a substantial amount of advanced full-time work, including some degree or sub-degree work, recruiting their students on a regional or, in some cases, on a national basis. Since 1966, many of these very large and important colleges have become poly-technics and have concentrated almost exclusively on degree and sub-degree courses for students over 18. This illustrates another source of confusion. The further education system at its top end has always included a considerable amount of degree work.

But the picture is becoming more complicated with two new developments; the bringing of the colleges of education (formerly known as teacher training colleges) into the field of further education, and the introduction of the two-year diploma of higher education (DipHE) into FE and else-where. Some colleges of education are combining with FE institutions, while others are diversifying their work. We shall look at this in more detail in Chapter 14. Even so, at the moment the top end of FE is buoyant and there are well over 200,000 students taking advanced courses at degree and sub-degree level.

Let us now, as we pick our way delicately through this tangled thicket, deal simply and briefly with the functions and aims of colleges of FE. Functions first.

A college of FE exists primarily to serve the needs of an advanced industrial society. It does this in three ways: first by promoting and providing full-time education, academic and vocational, at various levels for young people over 16 intending to proceed into industry, business, the professions, and higher education; secondly, by promoting and providing similar part-time courses during the day and evening for persons already in employment, irrespective of age; and, thirdly, by promoting and providing education for adults.

But I must qualify this. (This is one of the snags in writing about technical education. No sooner do you make these broad, comfortable statements than you immediately have to make finicking amendments.)

In recent years colleges of further education have taken on several subsidiary roles, and one of the most significant of these is in the field of general education. Here colleges are doing a rapidly increasing amount of orthodox GCE O and A level work for the 16-19 age group, with special emphasis on the preparation of students for entry to higher education and teacher training. We shall look at this development later on.

Add to this work the amount of general education contained in the curriculum of the full-time vocational courses and you can see why some feel that the title 'technical college' is almost becoming a misnomer. This is especially true of many local colleges where the development of full-time courses, both GCE and vocational, has been accompanied by a falling off in day-release courses. There has, in fact, been a marked and permanent shift towards full-time educational provision.

I have used the term 'vocational' several times and I think it might be helpful if I said a little more about it at this point. Historically the English do not love technical education and they love vocational courses even less. We honour vocations: we despise the vocational. And not only in England. In many countries 'vocational' is a dirty word and it is used contemptuously of those institutions engaged in such work. For us in FE, the term 'vocational' includes all education and training which leads to the acquisition of employable knowledge and skills. It thus embraces preparation for a variety of occupations ranging from medicine to sheet metalwork, from farming to electrical engineering, and from hotel management to plumbing. 'Vocational' does not equate with 'practical'.

Colleges have another major role which has emerged during the late 'sixties and this is the provision of education

B

for adults. Although this means primarily conventional adult education by means of evening classes, it also includes an increasing amount of adult training and re-training. As a result of colleges assuming the mantle of adult education, we have seen the development of the concept of the college as a cultural focus for the district it serves. Colleges have excellent facilities and are admirably placed to encourage music and the arts. Much depends here on the position of the college and the nature of its catchment area but many colleges are becoming lively and stimulating cultural centres and the term 'community colleges' is beginning to be heard.

Another function of the technical college, and one that is neither sufficiently publicised nor recognised, is that of a safety net to catch those who have lost their way in, fallen out of, or, in some cases, been ejected from, the educational system, public and private. Our role is that of the long-stop or sweeper-up—which partly accounts for the stimulating variety of our students.

We also provide a means of re-entry into the educational system for many young men and women who leave school between the ages of 16 and 18 to make their way in the world only to realise a year or so later that progress will be very difficult indeed unless they obtain extra qualifications or take certain vocational courses. Unable or unwilling to return to school, they turn to FE instead and are welcomed back into the fold.

For not only do we offer a second way, we also offer a second chance. It is not given to many of us in this life to wipe the slate clean and make a fresh start. Yet this is what the colleges offer to these young adults who have missed their footing or lost their sense of direction. Although we need to ensure students are suitably qualified to enter a course, once they are accepted it is then up to them. They may have had an undistinguished school record, they may have had one or two 'lost years' somewhere, or they may have had all kinds of personal problems but this is a new opportunity for them to make good. We are not interested in their past but only in what they can achieve with our help in the future. And the responsefulness is terrific!

For generations, the technical college acted as the centre of technical and scientific research in its area. This role has been reinforced in recent years by the research activities of certain large colleges and the billeting of industrial liaison officers in selected institutions. Industry and business are now coming to look upon colleges not only as educational institutions but as centres which can offer up-to-date professional help, theoretical and practical, on all kinds of highly specialised subjects and problems. It is also encouraging to see college libraries being used by enterprising firms as resource-centres where information and advice is immediately available.

The philosophy and educational aims of technical education are rarely discussed. Philosophy and technical education are curious bed-fellows anyway and I imagine that not all principals have a clear idea of the educational aims they are pursuing or the means by which those aims may be achieved. I imagine, too, there are relatively few principals who attempt to clarify ends and means to their teaching staff. So rapid has been our expansion, so pressing the problems of accommodation, staffing and equipment, so generally frantic the pace, that such niceties as educational aims have tended to be lost in the smoke and tumult of battle. In the bold, buccaneering days of rip-roaring expansion one sensed the unvoiced cry, 'Never mind the education, let's get on with developing the work'. Or am I being unkind?

Although my colleagues would naturally want to add a personal gloss, few would quibble with these four broad FE aims. First, to assist to the full the personal development of students, intellectually, physically, emotionally, and morally. This is one of the accepted aims of education in this country and one to which we in FE subscribe—though some of us are a bit behind with our subs. Secondly, to enable students to pass their examinations. I hope you will not think this traditional aim of ours an ignoble one, although it is a very narrow view and by itself would be intolerable. However, many students attend our courses at considerable personal inconvenience and often at some financial sacrifice on their part or on the part of their parents. They come with a specific objective and, if they are accepted for their course and work hard, they are entitled to our best efforts to help them realise their expectations. Thirdly, to educate students so that they can take their place easily in a rapidly evolving and increasingly technical society. Finally, we aim to produce future citizens who are sensible, confident, courteous and happy.

Such are our aims. How the colleges set out, consciously or unconsciously, to achieve them we shall examine in the course of this book.

CHAPTER THREE

The range of the work

Upon the education of the people of this country, the fate of this country depends.
Benjamin Disraeli, House of Commons
June 15, 1874

Take any part of the economy and you will almost certainly find it linked by education and training to a college of FE. This nationwide coverage is reflected in the extraordinary variety of our work which is the most baffling aspect of an FE college. The mind simply boggles. How shall I begin to convey it to you? In the first place you have to grasp the sheer academic span of our work. This ranges from craft, and GCE O level through ONC and A level right up to HNC and honours degree work. It is unusual nowadays for all these to be contained in one single college but they are all available within the further education system.

This is fairly straightforward. What is not so straight-forward to a wilting layman is the bewildering diversity of the courses run in the four sectors, industrial, commercial, professional, and academic in which we are active. In each of these four sectors there are both full-time and part-time courses and these are organised at various levels so that students can enter according to their qualifications and ability.

A mere catalogue of courses will tell you little, so I think the best way of giving you an idea of our range is to take you round a typical local/area college. Besides giving me a chance to tell you about the work done by the different departments, this Cook's tour will give you an impression of the inside of a modern college. Incidentally the college I have chosen (not Slyme Green) does not run any degree courses although it does offer one or two HNC and HND courses. This will make life a little simpler . . . It might also make things a little easier if I said something about the curious initials ONC (Ordinary National Certificate) and HNC (Higher National Certificate) which refer to the national certificate scheme upon which a large part of our technical education system is built. Established originally in 1921 for engineering, the scheme covers a number of subjects and provides a nationally recognised qualification through part-time study. There are two levels, ordinary and higher. To enter the ONC courses students must be over 16 and have four O levels or four CSE Grade 1's. The ONC is a two-year course and the standard is approximately A level. Having obtained their ONC, students may then proceed to the HNC course which entails a further two years of part-time study.

There are full-time courses available corresponding to ONC and HNC known as Ordinary National Diploma (OND) and Higher National Diploma (HND) which enable the curriculum to be dealt with in much greater depth. The OND courses last two years but with the rapid growth of sandwich courses* most HND courses now last three years. In fact, virtually all HNDs in engineering and half the HNDs in business studies are three-year sandwich courses. As a qualification the HND approaches the level of a degree.

I hope you have grasped that. I must now tell you that this system is about to be dismantled and phased out and the beginnings of a new one introduced as from September, 1976. All these certificates we have been discussing have come to be regarded in recent years as basically technician (ONC) and higher technician (HNC) qualifications. There has been considerable overlapping with the technician courses provided by the City and Guilds of London Institute and even within those courses there was already room for considerable rationalisation. Technician education, in short, presented a confusing and fragmented pattern and as a result the Technician Education Council (TEC) was set up in 1973 to carry out a major overhaul. Its brief was to develop a unified national system of courses for technicians at all levels in industry and elsewhere.

---

* See glossary.

Much of the work has now been done and within a few years technician students will be leaving colleges with one of the following TEC qualifications: Certificate, Diploma, Higher Certificate, Higher Diploma. Obviously there is some correspondence between the new qualifications and the old national certificate scheme but there are fundamental changes in course structure and examining methods which are just starting to register with college staff.

There is now also a Business Education Council (BEC) set up in 1974 to do much the same task for business education at sub-degree level but BEC is still very much at the chrysalis stage. Cynics may mutter, '*Plus ça change, plus c'est la même chose*'; but this attempt at a wholesale revision of technician courses and sub-degree business courses is one of the most important developments in FE of the 'seventies.

And so we come to Workwell Technical College. We will pretend that it is Saturday morning so that we can wander round undisturbed. Before we go up the drive, a brief word about the layout. You can see that it consists primarily of a multi-storey building much like a modern office block, with a smaller block linking it to a series of single-storey, factory-type buildings with their distinctive roof lights, stretching away at one side. In the tall building are housed the business studies, general education, and the hotel and catering departments, together with most of the administration. These are the 'clean' and 'non-noisy' areas. In this building they tried to have one department or section occupying a single floor but this arrangement broke down within two years of opening and there is now considerable blurring of the horizontal lines.

The engineering and building departments are contained in the extensive workshop area at the side and they are separated from the rest of the college for obvious reasons. They need special lighting, access and services, many items of equipment are large and heavy and much of the work done here is necessarily noisy and distracting. I am not saying this area is 'unclean' but oil, fumes and dust are the accompaniments and products of its activities. Most of the theoretical work of these departments is done in that square building at the rear of the workshops—you can just see the top of it.

Although you cannot make it out clearly from here because of the trees you can also see part of a substantial building close to the tower block. This is the main hall—cum theatre, cum examination hall, cum ballroom, cum exhibition hall, cum everything else. Because of its size and its well-equipped stage it is in great demand by local organisations for all kinds of activities.

Let us find out, therefore, which of these wretched glass doors is open and go into the foyer or main entrance hall. On the left is the enquiries desk with the college office and registrar's office behind it. To our right, behind more glass doors, is an administrative area with the vice-principal's room and the principal's sanctum. In this part all is peace and close carpeting. Here visitors, bottomed on black-buttoned couches, watch svelte secretaries undulate between the rubber plants.

We will start this morning by taking the lift up to the hotel and catering department on the top floor and then work our way down. The lift deposits us in a lobby which looks as though it belongs to the type of hotel we can so rarely afford to stay in. We pass through into the training restaurant where the lecturer in waiting, smartly dressed in black coat and striped trousers, supervises the service of food by his students. The restaurant is open to the public every weekday and, since the food and service are excellent and the charge is modest, you need to book your table early.

Possession of an hotel and catering department is something of a status symbol among principals. The restaurant, with a staffing ratio most West End establishments would envy, is ideal for entertaining our many visitors and for creating a favourable impression upon a hungry public. But principals have to be careful. The system ultimately rebels against a diet of *sole bonne femme*, *tournedos Rossini*, *coq au vin* and *crêpes Suzette*, so most ration themselves to one or two appearances a week. Even so their wives are envious.

We disappear through the double doors at the end into the gleaming and elaborate training kitchens—so very different, one feels, from the basement kitchens many of the students will encounter when they start work. Here, under the imperious eye of the chef instructor, students on the two-year full-time catering course get a thorough training in the preparation, cooking and presentation of food. Since Workwell is close to several resorts there is a steady demand for its students and an abundance of holiday jobs. There is a course, too, for those girls who wish to become book-keeper/receptionists.

Let us walk down the stairs to the department of business studies (it used to be called 'commerce') which is spread over the next two floors. Although in the larger cities the more advanced commercial work tends to be concentrated in the polytechnics, many colleges, Workwell included, still run HND and HNC courses for those aspiring to responsible positions in business. Like the others, Workwell also offers these courses at the ordinary level.

The OND is a two-year full-time course for 16 year olds with four GCE O level passes who are aiming at executive posts in commerce and industry. This excellent diploma, which is equivalent to A level, gives a thorough knowledge of the structure and functions of commerce and of typical business organisations and transactions. Besides being a valuable qualification in its own right, it enables students who pass well to enter degree courses at polytechnics and at most universities. It also gives exemptions from the intermediate examinations of most professional bodies.

Many successful OND students go on to the HND course where they are often joined by students coming straight in from school at 18 with at least one A level pass. At Workwell the HND is organised as a three-year sandwich course with special emphasis on data processing. Although the department has no computer of its own, it has access to one in the town thanks to the good relations the head of department has established with the firm. During the session it also runs a series of very popular short courses on computer appreciation and on the computer languages *Fortran* and *Basic*.

I see we are outside the typewriting rooms. You will notice these are wired for audio-typewriting and that there is a mixture of manual and electric typewriters in each room so that the girls can widen their experience. Workwell runs the usual range of full-time secretarial courses—the bread-and-butter work of the department—topped off by an intensive one-year post A level course which has proved popular with girls leaving the sixth forms of local schools.

But perhaps the most popular course of all is what we call the TOPS secretarial course. This is one of the many courses provided nationally through the Training Opportunities Scheme which was introduced in 1972 to improve training and retraining facilities for people over 19. Full-time courses last between twelve and twenty-four weeks, and are also offered in engineering and building, but it is the secretarial and clerical courses which have caught the imagination of the public, especially married women. The ladies know they are on to a good thing; during the course they receive an earnings related training allowance plus their travelling expenses, so it is an excellent example of 'Earn While You Learn'.

Further along this corridor is a well-equipped training office where students learn how to use the various types of duplicating, copying and accounting machines they will meet in the modern office and where they are trained in standard procedures in filing, and handling mail, and switchboard operation.

The department runs secretarial courses during the day and it also offers day-release courses for young people in the retail and distributive trades, for young office workers, and for new entrants to the civil service, local government and public boards. The ordinary national certificate in public administration has been geared to the needs of this last group and with its emphasis on government and the social services is proving most successful.

The business studies department is pretty active in the evenings, partly and regrettably because of the reluctance of banks, insurance companies and many commercial firms to give their employees day-release. Employees in these organisations have professional associations, like the Institute of Bankers and the Chartered Insurance Institute, whose examinations lead to membership and are the recognised route to promotion. There are similar bodies for accountants (pure and applied) and for company secretaries. However, the pattern is changing rapidly. Several professional bodies, led by the banks and insurance companies, have decided to abandon their individual examinations in favour of the national certificate schemes and are now starting to give day-release for ONC. The final examination for membership will still continue to be controlled by the professional bodies and is of degree standard. So Workwell, which currently offers a number of courses leading to the intermediate and final examinations of various professional bodies, expects to see a significant shift from evening to day work over the next few years and an increase in its ONC numbers.

The college also offers shorthand and typewriting classes as well as courses in works and office management and supervisory studies in the evenings.

Management education, by the way, is an established part of the work—'we are all managers now'—although it lacks the established course pattern of the older subjects. Much management education is carried out by short courses run during the day and evening and through the medium of one-day conferences on special topics, such as organisational theory or management by objectives. Further along this corridor, in fact, is a smart lecture theatre which is used a great deal by management students. Adjoining it are several seminar rooms, each seating up to about ten people where courses can be split up into small groups for detailed and controlled discussion.

At the far end of this corridor, beyond the lecture theatre, is a 24-booth language laboratory complete with sound-proof recording rooms, a tape store and a technician. This is the area where the department has been building up a reputation for crash courses in languages for busy executives.

It is time now for us to go below and visit the general education department. I have devoted a special chapter to this department and its activities later in the book so I will not bother you with too much detail here. Much of the accommodation on the next two floors consists of classrooms and the familiar physics, chemistry and biology laboratories of your youth. This department runs a wide range of full- and part-time GCE A and O level courses, particularly for the 16–19 age group. It also provides part-time courses in English for foreign students into which flaxen-haired *au pairs*, dark-eyed domestics, and volatile virgins of good family bring a welcome whiff of abroad.

This department looks after what are sometimes patronisingly referred to as women's subjects. It is always rather a problem in colleges to know under which banner to place courses like hairdressing, pre-nursing, residential care and hospital cadets. Sometimes nursing and hairdressing find a home in the science department (if there is one) or even with hotel and catering; quite often they are taken under the broad and well-disposed wing of the general education department. If you have sufficient students and courses, perhaps the best solution is to group them together and call them, for want of a more euphonious title, the department of Food, Fashion and Health.

There is a flourishing nursing course at Workwell and for the home economics element of their course the students use the beautifully equipped domestic science (DS) rooms on the next floor down. These DS rooms are also in use every evening because the department is responsible for all the non-vocational evening classes offered by the college—and cookery is a great favourite. With the facilities of the whole college at its disposal, Workwell is able to offer a most stimulating programme of leisure courses during the winter.

We are now among the ladies with a vengeance. At this corner, what looks like a smart bar turns out to be the reception area for the hairdressing course. The modern salon, like the training restaurant, is open to the public during the week and for a modest sum, the ladies of Workwell can have their hair shampooed and set, trimmed, tinted, permanently waved, or re-styled by the students on the two-year full-time course. The students are mainly girls but you do get the occasional lucky young man.

Down these stairs and we are back in the foyer again. There is no need for us to go outside to reach the technical departments because there is a corridor leading to them from the foyer. This takes us past the refectory which effectively links the vertical block we have just left to the horizontal workshop area. On the opposite side of the corridor to the refectory is the entrance to the sports hall which is a recent development of the standard gymnasium. Beyond the sports hall lie the college playing fields, stretching away towards the housing estate in the distance.

Because of the nature of our work, engineering departments have always been the largest departments in colleges, although this supremacy is now being challenged in many colleges by the rapid rise of departments of general education. In many cases they grew so unwieldy that they had to be split. This used to be done along the traditional division into mechanical and electrical engineering but principals found a more convenient division was often a horizontal one, with professional and technician courses in one department and the predominantly craft courses in another. This is the case at Workwell.

You will find me referring so often in this book to craft apprentices and to technicians, and to craft and technician level courses that I had better explain these terms as we walk along. They are common to engineering and building and are now spilling over into other fields.

By craft apprentice, we mean a young man whose job is primarily a practical one and who will eventually become a skilled craftsman at the end of his period of apprenticeship and training. He takes a craft course at college which is designed to supplement his practical training in industry. If he is in mechanical engineering for example, he will develop his skills in fitting and in operating standard machine tools like lathes, shapers and millers. He will also continue to do a certain amount of mathematics, science and drawing.

It is not quite so easy to define 'technician' because this term is applied to numerous jobs of a responsible and supervisory nature in industry involving a much higher level of technical knowledge and communication skills than that needed by a craftsman. The technician is usually a young man or woman who left school with a few O levels or CSE passes. He must be reasonably good at maths and science because these two subjects are the most important in his course. Technician courses are quite demanding and in the final year the standard approximates to A level and in parts exceeds it.

But I smell coolant, that distinctive all-pervading smell, which means we have reached the engineering workshops. All day and every evening this area swarms with day-release lads who form the majority of the engineering students. I think this part of the college, with its specialist accommodation, best gives you an idea of the diversity of the work and the range of subjects studied in a large department.

The craft department runs the usual range of day-release craft courses. Stretching away down this corridor are its various workshops: fitting shops, machine shops, shops for welding and fabrication (formerly known as sheet metal work), and shops for electrical craft practice and electrical installation. At the far end are two large motor vehicle workshops and a further shop devoted to panel beating and bodywork repairs. This is where the apprentices carry out the practical part of their craft courses and where the technician and senior students come to do their workshop technology.

Although most of this department's students are part-time, it also runs full-time courses. As a result of the Industrial Training Act, the Engineering Industry Training Board (EITB) has developed in collaboration with the colleges a full-time forty-eight week 'off-the-job' training course. ('Off-the-job' means away from the production line or from production needs.) This has now become the standard basic course for first year school-leavers entering general engineering. After this first year there is a developing system of module training under which apprentices take units of training and further education related to their employment. Workwell also offers a full-time course lasting twenty-four weeks for apprentices in the garage trade, run in conjunction with the Road Transport Industry Training Board.

I have just mentioned two of the training boards set up under the Industrial Training Act. Before we go any further I think it would be helpful if I told you something about this

Act which has had far-reaching effects upon the colleges. I see the head of department's door is open, let us take the weight off our feet in his office for a few minutes.

The Act came into being in 1964 as a result of mounting dissatisfaction with the training in industry and commerce. This was poor by any standard and appalling by comparison with our economic rivals in Western Europe. In a few industries (catering is an example) training was pretty well non-existent. The training and education of a skilled, adaptable and inventive work force is vital for economic development and we were slowly becoming aware that the pool of skilled manpower was insufficient for our needs.

The Industrial Training Act had three main objectives: to ensure an adequate supply of properly trained men and women at all levels in industry; to secure an improvement in the quality and efficiency of industrial training; and to share the cost of training more evenly between the firms.

To achieve these highly desirable ends the Act gave the then Ministry of Labour power to set up industrial training boards. Twenty-four boards covering such sectors as engineering, hotel and catering, distributive trades, printing and publishing, road transport, shipbuilding, chemical and construction industries have been established, and with six boards operating under other provisions, nearly three-quarters of industry now comes within the scope of a training board.

A board has two main duties: first, to make sure that sufficient training is provided and, secondly, to publish recommendations on such matters as the nature, content, and the length of training for occupations in their industry, together with the further education which should be associated with this training. And all this with economic and technical changes very much in mind.

Lest you start identifying the boards with craft training, I should make it clear that the powers of a board extend to all forms of training (and re-training) from operative through supervisory right up to management level. The boards naturally concentrated on the training of apprentices (you have to start somewhere!) and there is general agreement that their development of first year off-the-job apprentice training has proved the most successful and valuable of their activities.

The two boards which have made the biggest impact on colleges so far are the Construction Industry Training Board (CITB) and the EITB. The latter is not only the largest of the boards, covering some three million workers in the industry, but was the first one to get off the ground and set the pace and pattern for the others.

At the start, some colleges felt an understandable reluctance to become identified with low-level courses with a high 'training' content but, after some teething trouble, work for the training boards soon became part and parcel of the colleges' standard programme.

The training boards have been going for just over a decade. As a result of the Employment and Training Act of 1973 they now find themselves under the banner of the Training Services Agency (TSA), one of the two executive branches of the Manpower Services Commission. The TSA is responsible for training carried out in sectors of employment covered by ITBs, for training carried out under TOPS, for the unemployed, and also for training in sectors not covered by ITBs, although in the last category its authority is less well defined. The TSA is thus responsible for the whole of the country's training effort. It faces many problems and its efforts to solve them will impinge directly on colleges of further education.

Although there is no doubt that the training boards have raised the quality of the long-term training being given to young people, the boards have been less successful in increasing the actual volume of training. Moreover, they have been unable to do much about the lack of training given to hundreds of thousands of young people entering certain industries and occupations.

As far as an apprentice training in engineering and construction is concerned, sanctions against uncooperative and reluctant employers have not proved effective and there remains the problem of the many thousands of small firms which are still outside the scope of the boards. When both

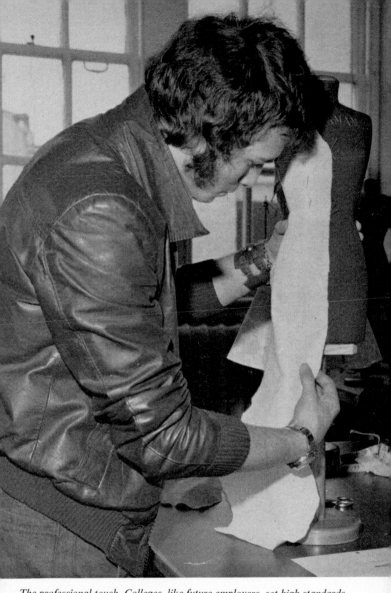

The professional touch. Colleges, like future employers, set high standards.

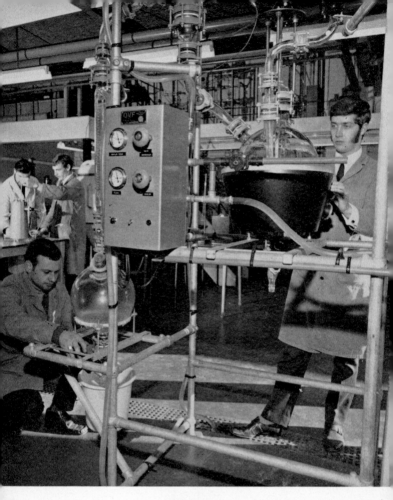

Colleges provide specialist accommodation and equipment to allow students maximum scope in their work.

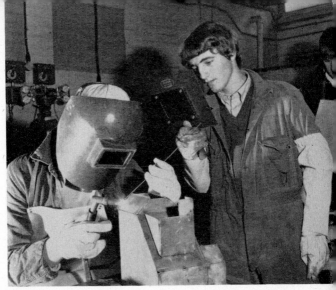

Note the protective clothing. Colleges always instil safe working practice.

Skilled men of tomorrow. The many day-release courses for craft apprentices and technicians, together with their training in industry, ensure that high standards are achieved.

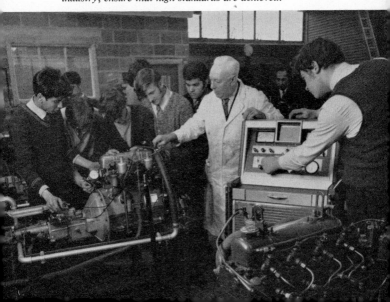

Building students busily acquiring their craft skills.

Audio-typewriting, a time-saving technique popular with busy executives, is an important element in the secretarial course for students with a good command of English.

There is more to office skills than knowing how to change a typewriter ribbon . . . the intricacies of the litho-machine are demonstrated.

The model shop helps the tutor to explain different approaches to retailing.

A glimpse of the reality for catering students in the training restaurant which is open to the public.

Art courses develop creative skills for individual work and introduce students to the design techniques used in mass-production.

stick and carrot fail, it is not easy to see what measures will be effective in increasing the volume of training at a time of recession and unemployment.

This is the major problem that the TSA and the ITBs will have to grapple with during the next few years. One proposal being discussed at present is that the cost of apprentice training, particularly first year training, might be centrally funded with the financial burden being shared in some way between the employers and the suffering tax-payer. This is delicate, politically, and the powers-that-be are naturally cautious about it.

Sombre thoughts for a Saturday morning! Let us arise and shake off dull care and go and see the other engineering department which is responsible for technician courses (that is, ONC and technician) and higher technician courses (HNC).

This corridor on our left leads us to the building which contains the specialist laboratories used by the technician students for the experiments and investigations which form an integral part of their studies. Here we find labs for physics, heat engines, mechanics, hydraulics, strength of materials, telecommunications, electronics, instrument technology, and electrical engineering. There is also that holy of holies, the metrology lab, which contains all the expensive precision measuring equipment. On the first floor there are two spacious drawing offices equipped with both drawing tables and drafting machines. Technical drawing, like mathematics and applied mechanics, is one of the fundamentals of engineering and some knowledge of it is necessary for all those working in the industry. The craftsman on the workshop floor, for example, must be able to read blueprints and if he can sketch freehand, quickly and intelligibly, so much the better.

Workwell runs technician courses in both mechanical and electrical engineering and also in telecommunications, motor vehicle work, and instrument measurement and control. There is a well-supported ONC course and from this springs an HNC in mechanical engineering which with the HND in business studies, is the highest level course run by the college.

If we retrace our steps to the workshops and go down the

C

corridor beyond the motor vehicle section we find ourselves in the building department. You can always tell when you are near the building department by the ear-splitting din coming from the plumbing workshop where well-built lads are thumping great lumps of lead with curious wooden tools called bossing sticks. The brickwork shop hardly resembles the library of the Athenaeum either.

This department has many affinities with its bigger engineering neighbours. Here apprentices learn the three basic building crafts, bricklaying, plumbing, and carpentry and joinery. At the end of the course the students sit their City and Guilds examination. City and Guilds is short for City and Guilds of London Institute (CGLI) which is the national examining body for all craft and technician courses—and its enormous list of examination subjects makes illuminating reading.

The building department is not concerned exclusively with craft courses for it, too, runs an ONC course for the abler lads. For his HNC in building and for the higher flights of building education, a young man would normally have to travel to a specialist college of building or to a polytechnic. The specialist college would also cater for boys leaving school at 16 or 18 who wish to become architects, building and quantity surveyors, or go in for estate management or town and country planning.

Hidden from the road and just beyond the main workshop area is another range of single-storey buildings housing the studios and workshops of the art department—sometimes known for historical and sentimental reasons as the school of art.

Art education has two main branches. First there is fine art, by which is meant painting and sculpture—or three-dimensional design (3D) as it is now called. The senior fine art course is called the foundation course, a one-year diagnostic course for students aged 17 who have five O levels. Students who wish to become artists, teachers and designers are prepared for entry to colleges of art where they take a three-year course leading to a BA (Hons) degree in art and design.

And then there is the other branch of art known as vocational design. Departments usually offer a variety of courses including advertising design, photography, interior design, technical illustration, dress design, typography and textile design. Workwell offers several of these, specialising in advertising design. Because several of the teachers are active practitioners and have many contacts in the industry its students find little difficulty in obtaining first posts as junior designers or studio technicians in advertising agencies or in industry. A very popular course with girls is the one in dress and their work comes very much to the fore in the fashion parade which is the highlight of the annual open day. Workwell is fortunate in having a range of painting and design studios as well as well-equipped specialist rooms for pottery, screen printing, photography and 3D.

Much of the work in art, particularly screen-printing and pottery, is dusty and messy and so are most of the materials —paint, plaster of paris, clay, inks, etc. You soon realise that art is very much a craft operating under craft conditions.

The department has two other strings to its bow. It offers a popular programme of recreational afternoon and evening classes to which many adults, including a number of local amateur artists, return year after year, while a sterner note is struck by the day-release classes it runs for lads in the painting and decorating business.

Well, that's about as far as we go. If you're anything like me, by this time your feet are aching and every fibre of your being is crying out for refreshment. Luckily the King's Head is just down the road where raven-haired Ruby bends prettily over the pumps. There we can have a convivial word about the students. The college may be like a tomb today but on Monday it will be humming and pulsating like a busy hive.

CHAPTER FOUR

The students

Under that Almighty Fin
The littlest fish may enter in.

Heaven Rupert Brooke

Through our glass doors streams a bewildering mixture of students. They are of all ages, from 16 to 80, and they come in all shapes and sizes, from small men's to ladies' outsize. In many parts of the country they now come in several races and a range of colours. They spring from a variety of backgrounds, come from different types of schools, and from a multiplicity of occupations.

I never tire of saying to people that a college of FE is a world in microcosm. This is a telling phrase with its vague scientific smack, since few are quite sure what a microcosm is. I then come down an octave and stress we are the only true comprehensive institution. At this, eyes light up, and in some cases fervour appears. I emphasise the ability range. Under our extensive wing we shelter students who are reading for an honours degree as well as the first year engineering apprentice, covered in coolant and shin-deep in swarf.

I also emphasise the age range; from the school leaver of 16 taking a commercial course to the oldest old-age-pensioner in the business who comes every Thursday night as regular as clockwork for her dressmaking class. And I dwell upon that recent phenomenon, the wide social range.

Do not run away, however, with the impression that our student body consists of an army of teenagers supplemented by a horde of pensioners attending evening classes. This is not the whole story. True, most of our full-time and day-release students are aged 16 to 21 and there is a significant number of people over 60 attending non-vocational evening classes. But there are thousands of young men and women in their early 20s on HND or degree courses as well as a great number in the 25–45 bracket attending short courses.

Few of our full-time students are married, but this happy state is not uncommon among the day-release students. The age of apprenticeship is still generally 16 to 21 and many of the older apprentices on the final stages of their courses are married. The other day I came across an apprentice not quite 18 who was not only married but had two children.

The public find it hard to understand our categories of student. This is hardly surprising because most people naturally think of education in terms of full-time attendance. We who have grown old and grey in technical education fling about expressions like 'sandwich student' or 'day-release student' without realising that these terms are almost meaningless to those outside FE. So let me make all blindingly clear by letting you meet some of the typical young men and women in your local college.

Let us make a start with the easy ones, the ones we can all understand, the full-time students. These are young adults aged between 16 and 22.

Michael (18): 'I went to a secondary modern school and came out with four O levels and a couple of CSEs. My dad's a bus driver but I wanted something better than that. I like meeting people so I thought of business. My headmaster advised me to apply for the OND course in Business Studies at the college. I'm just finishing my second year now. I've been accepted as a trainee manager by one of the biggest multiples so my future looks pretty good.'

Margaret (16): 'My sister's a private secretary and I've always wanted to work in an office. I left my comprehensive school when I was 16 because it didn't run a proper commercial course. I'm doing a two-year secretarial course at the college. We do audio-typewriting and there is a model office where we learn how to work all the latest machines. When I leave I hope to start as a shorthand typist in an insurance firm. In two or three years I hope to be a private secretary too.'

Ann (18): 'I took my O levels at the local grammar school but they couldn't offer me the A level subjects I wanted. So I applied to the college. I want to go to university to read veterinary science but this is not going to be terribly easy because there are far more applicants than places. If I don't get a university place I shall apply to an agricultural college to take a national diploma in agriculture.'

Peter (19): 'I was quite good at art at school and I used to go to the Saturday morning classes run by the School of Art. I saw some of the design and advertising layouts done by the graphics students and this set me off. I'm in the final year of the graphic design course myself now. My special interest is in photography and product illustration. When I leave I hope to work in an advertising agency. If you're really good you can do finished artwork on the roughs approved by the clients. I think one day I'd like to have a small business of my own.'

Frank (17): 'My father's a miner and he wanted me to learn a proper trade. He didn't want me to go down the pit. I didn't fancy it much either. It was the careers officer who really put me onto this course. He got me an apprenticeship with an engineering firm on the trading estate here—welding specialists they are. They sent me to the tech on this industrial training course. It lasts forty-eight weeks and you learn how to use a lathe and a shaper and a miller. They teach you gas and electric arc welding too. The teachers aren't too bad. They can clamp down if they need to. My favourite subject is technical drawing. I always liked drawing at school and I think I'd like to be a draughtsman.'

Abdulrazzak Hussein (18): 'I came here from Iran. I went to a state school in Tehran and gained my school leaving certificate—which is roughly equivalent to your GCE O level —in nine subjects. I wanted to be a civil engineer so I thought of coming to England because a Western European degree is highly valued in my country. Some of my friends were here already and they advised me to take my A levels at a college of further education to gain university entrance. I'm now doing physics, maths and engineering drawing, and enjoying the course very much. Soon after I arrived, the college accommodation officer—she is a very nice lady—helped me find a small flat. There are several other Arab students in the college and I see them a lot in the evenings, but I get on well with the other English students in my group. I'm very keen on basketball and I've been playing regularly for the college team. I like life here in England and I'm looking forward to going to a university or polytechnic next year.'

John (19): 'I took my A levels at school but my grades weren't good enough to get me a place at university. So I'm taking history, economics and sociology at college. I like it here. You get a lot of freedom but you learn to work hard on your own. I hope to go to university later this year to read geography and eventually I should like to work as a town planner.'

Next we come to part-time students. As we have seen, these have always been one of the features of technical education. There are two kinds: part-time day and part-time evening. We'll take the part-time day student first. In this country technical education is closely related to a well-established apprenticeship system which reaches right back to the craft guilds in the Middle Ages. Most of the apprentices in our colleges are drawn from the engineering and construction industries. During the early summer these industries recruit apprentices from school-leavers aged 16. The following September these young workers are released one day per week (with pay!) by their employers to attend courses of education and training, appropriate to their employment and future, at the local college. We usually refer to these lads as day-release students and the part-time courses they attend as day-release courses.

For many years the standard apprenticeship lasted five years, from 16 to 21. This has become much less rigid now it is recognised that this period of apprenticeship does not necessarily coincide with the amount of training and experience required for a particular skilled trade. Today it is usually three or four years before an apprentice or trainee is recognised as a skilled craftsman and in that time he will attend the college one day per week, receiving, we hope, his craft, technician, or national certificate at the end of his course.

Incidentally, our system of day-release has few parallels in Western Europe and there are only the slightest traces of it in the United States. It is a nineteenth century development based on the idea that practical and theoretical work for the apprentice should go hand-in-hand. What the apprentice learns at college (mainly theory) is confirmed, strengthened and developed by his practical experience on the workshop floor, in the drawing office, or on site. And there is something to be said educationally for this arrangement.

Of course, not all our day-release students are male and come from the engineering and construction industries. Hundreds of thousands of young employees, male and female, are released to college from every part of the economy for appropriate part-time courses. They come from shops, offices, local government, hospitals, agriculture, and from a host of manufacturing and service industries.

Bill (19): 'I was fed up at school. I was in the C stream all the time. Dead boring, so I left to work in a garage—big Ford main dealers. I've always been mad on cars. They sent me to the tech one day a week. I didn't like the idea much. I wasn't very good at maths or science at school, so I messed about a bit at the start—you know. But it's sort of different now, somehow. One or two of the teachers are a bit hard, but they know their stuff. I'm in my third year now and I take my City and Guilds Motor Vehicle Craft Studies Certificate this summer. I run an old Cortina 1500. Me and my mate stripped it right down. It needs a respray but it goes like a bomb. Pow!'

Linda (17): 'I've always wanted to be a nurse. I've got four small brothers and sisters and I often look after them when my mum and dad go out. I did CSE at school and I was a house captain and a prefect. I thought of taking a prenursing course at the college of further education but I'd had enough of school. Besides, all my friends are working and there's not much money coming in at home. Then I heard about this cadet scheme from Mrs Carter, our careers teacher. I went to see matron at the infirmary and she accepted me. I have a proper cadet uniform and I get nearly £23 a week. I go to the college two days a week and at the end of the year I'm taking three O levels. I work at the hospital for the rest of the week. It's great. I'd like to go in for children's nursing after I get my SRN.'

Stewart (16): 'I was quite good at maths and drawing at school and the careers officer helped me get a job as a junior draughtsman in a local architect's office. Now I'm at the college on the construction technicians course. It's a four-year course with a pretty high standard. I think I'd like to become an architect's assistant. Later on I wouldn't mind working for one of the nationalised industries where there's a lot of variety in the work.'

Tony (20): 'I left my comprehensive school at 16 with two O levels and some CSEs. I was interested in engineering and model-making so I got an apprenticeship with this aircraft company. My dad's a fitter there. I got a good practical training in the works school and they sent me to classes at the local tech. I found the maths a bit tough but eventually I passed my ONC all right. I'm in the drawing office now and getting on well. I'm doing my HNC at the college of technology. My ambition? I think I'd like to be a planning engineer. I wouldn't mind doing some evening class teaching later on either. Me, a teacher!'

There is a more sophisticated type of day-release known as 'block-release'. Under this arrangement, the number of hours an apprentice would normally spend during the session on day-release is concentrated into one or more 'blocks' of attendance. These may last for as little as three weeks or for as long as eighteen weeks but this scheme usually enables the college to have the students for a little longer than ordinary day-release. There are many in FE who contend that for the more able student block-release has positive advantages and this argument is supported by a comparison of examination results achieved by students of roughly the same ability on day-release and on block-release. Block-release wins pretty convincingly, but not all would support it for the average craft apprentice who finds intensive periods of continuous study difficult to take. Block-release, by the way, is not restricted to work of craft level and to engineering alone. The system is used at all levels and in industries as different as building, catering and printing.

Keith (17): 'I got interested in radio and telecommunications at school. I left at 16 with five O levels and the careers officer got me an apprenticeship with the Post Office. I think they have one of the best training schemes in the country. In September the Post Office sent me to the college on this block-release course. I'm doing the first half of my ONC in engineering this year and I also learn telephony and telegraphy. I have two more blocks next year. If I get my ONC, I hope to go on and take my HNC and become an electrical engineer. Telecomms is expanding rapidly and there is plenty of scope for promotion.'

I think we are on more familiar ground when we turn to the part-time evening students. There are two main kinds; the leisure students and those taking vocational courses. Indeed you may well be one of the millions of students who pour in each autumn to take a quite astonishing variety of leisure courses—non-vocational classes is the title we often give to them. This is where we find the majority of our older students and these evening classes are the part of the college's work the public knows best. If you mention FE or the college, many people still associate it automatically with evening classes, with dressmaking and pottery and so on. Actually, although a local college may have several thousand non-vocational students, they only account for about 5 per cent of its work—which surprises most people. The bulk of our work is now done during the day.

Mrs S. (28): 'I come here every Thursday evening for a dressmaking class. This is really my only night out during the week. Bert looks after the two kiddies. It's a bit of a rush to get them ready for bed and get here by 7 o'clock but I manage it somehow. We've got about fourteen in the class which means you can get individual attention. The teacher's a very nice person, very friendly, and several of the students have been coming to her class for years. We have a break for a cup of tea at about 8 o'clock—it's more like a sort of club really. Every year, just before Easter, we have a fashion parade in the hall. You know, a proper catwalk and everything. Next year I hope to go onto tailoring. I make all my own clothes and my little girl's dresses. It saves me quite a bit.

Most of the students taking vocational courses are found in the Business Studies Department. Many are studying professional subjects such as law, accountancy, statistics and economics but they are greatly outnumbered by the girls and married women who are busy with shorthand, typewriting and English one or two evenings a week. In many cases the girls have taken a full-time secretarial course at the college and are now coming in for a further year to increase their speeds. Some girls (though not so many now that commercial courses are being offered in schools) are starting from scratch and will be attending college for two or three years until their stamina gives out or their boy friends become more demanding.

While we are talking of examination courses we must not forget the adults and teenagers who come in during the evening to take GCE O and A levels. Sometimes they do this for interest or intellectual stimulus but more often they are seeking qualifications for promotion or for entry to a particular course of training. And many adults are now able to attend part-time during the day.

Mrs B. (30): 'I left school at 15. I started work as an office junior and I went to night school twice a week for typing classes. I got married when I was 21 and I had to give up work when my son was born two years later. I now have two boys and I've become very interested in education. I'm a keen member of the PTA and I help with the Road Safety Club at the school. Some time ago I had this idea of qualifying myself for a new career when the boys were older. So I took the plunge and did an evening class in English Language O level—and I passed first time! Now I am taking a combined A and O level programme. I enjoy it here. Most of us in my group are married women and the college arranges the classes so we can start at 10 a.m. and finish in time to collect our children from school. All being well, I hope to take a teacher-training course next year, or some kind of social work training. I haven't made my mind up yet.'

Then we have the curiously named 'sandwich' students. These are usually students doing advanced work such as HNDs or CNAA degrees. The courses last three or four years and are arranged so that students spend alternate periods of varying length in college and working in industry or commerce. Again, the idea behind this scheme is to re-inforce theory with practical experience and the value of this arrangement is widely recognised.

Roger (20): 'I went to grammar school and in the sixth form I took physics, maths and applied maths. One day I saw a leaflet from British Rail offering a kind of one-week residential course at Derby. The men on my dad's side of the family have always worked on locos. I suppose I've inherited some of this. Anyway I went there and I enjoyed it. I felt this was for me. I had thought of going to university but I decided to apply to be taken on by BR as a sandwich student. I got good A levels and now I'm on a four-year sandwich course. This leads to a degree in mechanical engineering. During my first three years I spend six months at the college of tech-nology and six months at various railway works. The final year I spend full-time in college. I'm not quite sure what I want to do, but I think it will probably be something in research and development.'

And so we come to the last in our catalogue of students—the short course students. These may attend the college during the day or evening for vocational courses lasting as little as half a day or as long as one day per week for twelve weeks. These short courses cover every conceivable field and are often tailored to the requirements of a specific firm, for example, the foremen of an aircraft company, or the junior executives of an oil company, or a particular group of people, such as shop stewards or personnel officers. They bring into our colleges adults from every sort of background and occupation and help to give our institutions their unique flavour. We have supervisors, training officers, secretaries, police officers, librarians, and businessmen mixing with our full-time and day-release students.

Mrs J. (27), *ward sister:* 'I'm in charge of women's surgical at the Infirmary. Hospitals are very management conscious these days, and all the sisters from my group have been sent off to the college on this first-line management course. We do one day a week for twelve weeks. I've enjoyed coming back to college. I used to be a cadet here several years ago. I feel I've got a lot out of this course. We were all a bit shy to start with but it didn't last long and I found it interesting to compare notes with colleagues from other hospitals. The future? Well, I was married last March. My husband teaches handicapped children and we're hoping to emigrate to Canada next year. I plan to go on working and I think I'd like to qualify as a health visitor over there eventually.'

Our full-time students in the 16–19 age range come to us from all kinds of schools: secondary modern schools, grammar schools, comprehensive schools, and independent schools. And we can add to the mixture the students from overseas, especially young men from the Middle East and South-East Asia, which most colleges contain.

Many colleges are now receiving boys and girls aged 16 and upwards from public and private schools. For many parents the cost of keeping their children at independent schools after the age of 16 has become prohibitive. Faced with bleak reality they are forced to bring their sons and daughters home and to cast round for other ways of continuing their education—with careers and O and A levels very much in mind. The idea of going to the local comprehensive school does not attract these young people, but going to college does. The college, with its atmosphere of personal responsibility and purposiveness, appeals strongly to both parent and student. Besides, it's cheap! There are no fees to pay for the under 19s and to find something that is both cheap and first-class is an unusual combination these days.

I often wonder how our full-time students find their way into FE. Certainly some come to it by curious and wondrous chances. Yet the DES plays its part manfully enough by posting direct to careers teachers in all secondary schools bundles of 'Choose Your Course' information sheets dealing with post-school education and emphasising opportunities in FE. Similarly a number of LEAs produce leaflets which are sent to all their secondary schools indicating opportunities at 16-plus in both FE and schools. Many boys and girls in comprehensive and secondary modern schools

obviously receive information, advice and encouragement
from their headteachers and careers teachers—but much
depends upon the outlook and digestion of the headteacher.
I doubt whether pupils in the grammar schools are given any
information about us at all in a regular way. The odd college
or DES leaflet may creep into the library, like some subver-
sive tract, but that's about all.

We do not recruit large numbers from the grammar
schools since most of the boys and girls who decide to continue in full-time education after 16 will naturally stay on in
the sixth form. Many of these pupils are bound for the
universities and colleges of education, but we can be pretty
certain that most of those who fall by the wayside would
have been far better off taking an appropriate vocational
course at a college of further education. A few brave spirits
transfer to take their A levels with us because we can sometimes offer a wider and more flexible choice of A level subjects than their own grammar school—but it takes some doing.

We shall meet this situation later in the book so I shall
merely content myself here by stating there are now several
agencies, national and local, by which the opportunities in
FE are being made known to grammar school pupils. Of
course, as the process of comprehensive reorganisation nears
completion, so the grammar schools will wither on the bough
and in the future nearly all our full-time students will be
recruited from non-selective schools.

Many pupils in non-selective schools may receive their
first real information about FE from the local careers officer.
The careers officer's work tends to be undervalued by a
public unaware of its skilled nature. I always like to give the
careers officers a boost and I do so here because the careers
officer is a principal's best friend.

Careers guidance in the schools has changed a great deal
over the last few years. The idea of a general talk in the
pupils' penultimate year followed by an interview in the
final year is becoming outmoded. In many areas we now
find the emphasis being placed on the concept of careers
education. This is seen as a continuing process from the
third year onwards involving curriculum options, infor-

mation about the world of work and the range of careers, plus the traditional careers guidance element. To this process a variety of staff, besides the careers officer and the careers teacher, make their contribution.

In authorities with a progressive careers service the general talk in the fourth year has been superseded by group work and it may be here that the opportunities in FE are voiced for the first time. If not, they will certainly be discussed during the pupil's individual interview with the careers officer in his last year, when the pupil's interests and ambitions are reviewed and the careers officer, on the basis of his school record, seeks to point him in the appropriate direction. It is often at this stage that the opportunities in FE, hitherto mentioned in only a general way, crystallise into a decision to take a vocational course at the college. The careers officers are instrumental in channelling hundreds of thousands of boys and girls into our colleges every year. Can you wonder we are fond of them?

Many in FE feel that the quality of the careers guidance offered to pupils in the schools should be improved—and improved quickly. It still varies from the very good to the vestigial, despite the work of careers officers and the enthusiastic contribution, often in difficult conditions, of careers teachers in the schools. Everyone connected with education agrees that more resources should be made available for careers education, yet in our present parlous state there seems little chance of any significant expansion of the careers service, while staffing economies in the schools may reduce the effectiveness of careers teachers there.

Incidentally, the careers service is also responsible for careers guidance for students in colleges, whether they are full-time or day-release students. Careers offices have been established as part of, or attached to, certain colleges while other colleges have appointed staff specifically for careers education. But I do not think that we are yet paying sufficient attention to careers guidance in FE. It needs to be better organised and considerably extended. We tend to think, not unnaturally, that day-release students who are already in employment do not need it, and those taking full-time vocational courses have already decided what they want to do anyway. This is only true of the latter in a limited sense because they still need guidance within their chosen sector of employment. It also completely excludes the hundreds of thousands of young people on GCE courses who are in exactly the same position as sixth formers at school. So there is much to be done.

Actually many pupils may already have a shrewd idea of what the college has to offer. They may have been in a group that has toured the college, or they may have been taken there to an open day or to a play or concert. Again, these youngsters may well have brothers, sisters and friends who have taken full-time courses at the tech or who are attending as part-time students. Personal recommendation and the bush telegraph are potent factors and it is remarkable how soon news of a good thing gets around. The drums can also beat out quite a different story.

What is the attraction of the college of FE today for so many young people? I am confining myself here to full-time students because our day-release students attend for the best of all possible reasons—they are sent by their employers. We have seen how the college offers full-time students the courses they want, whether it is a vocational course leading towards a specific career or a GCE course which will enable them to obtain qualifications to proceed to higher education or to qualify for training in a chosen field. But there's more to it than this. It is the special adult atmosphere of the college that is the magnet and this atmosphere is a compound of several elements, efficacious in almost every case.

Apart from the social cachet of 'going to college', it is this adult atmosphere that intrigues young people. They have left school behind them and they are going into a 'grown-up' world where they will be mixing with adults and where they know they will be treated as young adults. Colleges recognise that the young people coming to them are physically adult. Even if they are still immature in other ways, how can you treat them except as young adults—especially as 18 year olds now have the vote?

Linked with this adult atmosphere is the highly popular

and publicised 'freedom' our students enjoy. Its more obvious manifestation to boys and girls coming in straight from school is an exhilarating absence of regulations and petty restrictions. There is no keeping to the left in the corridors and no attempt to stop them leaving the premises during the lunch hour. There is no question of uniform and there are no regulations regarding those vexing matters, dress and hair. Our students are also allowed to smoke—in certain places. When I talk to my new students like a father at the beginning of the session, I make the point that it is an expensive way to go but the decision is entirely theirs.

Now you know something of the age range of our student population you will appreciate the reasons for the absence of formal regulations and for the optional nature of many of our activities. You cannot cater for a large number of people over 18 and have it otherwise. Ours is an adult society. Naturally there are a few rules and regulations but these are only designed for social convenience so that staff and students in a busy organisation can get on with their work quietly and purposively in buildings which are often too crowded for comfort.

And college freedom works! It is surprising how quickly nearly all our students settle down in this informal environment. For a few of the younger ones it is such a heady experience that it sometimes takes them a couple of months before they adjust to this new way of life, but it rarely takes longer.

If our students are given a good deal of personal freedom, colleges emphasise that with such freedom goes personal responsibility for both work and conduct. This is the other side of the picture and one that is equally successful. In such an environment young people rapidly mature and become responsible. For those who are going on to higher education or further training, it is an excellent introduction to the attitudes and habits of work which will be expected from them.

I said earlier that one of the functions of a college is to offer a second chance, a new beginning, and I never fail to stress this opportunity. Some of our students from non-

D

selective schools have not done very well in the past but it is surprising and gratifying to find how many of these blossom out during their first year at college. With increasing confidence in tackling their work, there comes a welcome maturity in outlook and behaviour. You may argue that such maturity would have come in any case. I can only say how encouraging it is to see these youngsters develop into keen and hard-working students after a few months in a more informal and more realistic community.

I am using that word 'realistic' again. It keeps breaking in and it is significant. Students appreciate that the world of the FE college is rooted in reality. After all, most of them come to us for vocationally-biased courses. They know what they want to do and become, the subjects they have to study, the qualifications they must obtain. I think many of us in education who have tolerably orthodox backgrounds underestimate the desire among young adults to get to grips with the business of living. They want to see a more direct connection between education and life, and they are much more influenced by vocational considerations than students of twenty years ago.

This is why students appreciate the qualifications and experience gained in the world outside by many of the staff in FE. This is the basis of the rather special relationship between staff and students we shall come across in the next chapter.

We have dealt with the students: now it is the turn of the teachers.

CHAPTER FIVE

The teachers

We go upon the practical mode of teaching, Nickleby; the
regular education system. C-l-e-a-n, clean, verb active, to make
bright, to scour. W-i-n, win, d-e-r, winder, a casement.
When the boy knows this out of the book, he goes and does it.
Nicholas Nickleby Charles Dickens

FE teachers have a special advantage.

You see, most teachers in primary and secondary education have gone straight from school to a college of education (or teacher-training college) or to a university. They have then returned to the schools to take up their first teaching posts without ever having had the chance of acquiring experience of commercial or industrial life.

This is not the case with the majority of staff in colleges of FE. They are recruited from all levels in industry, commerce and the professions. We have works managers, mechanics, accountants, local government officers, sales directors, plumbers, chemical engineers—the list is as varied as the courses offered in the college.

I must stress that these men and women coming to us from the world outside possess the professional and technical qualifications appropriate to their calling. Many thousands of them possess degrees or degree equivalents in fields outside the traditional areas of BA or BSc. It is only their unfamiliarity that is misleading. It is because of this that some in the schools regard us as educational Daleks, creatures from another planet, with strange qualifications and stranger backgrounds.

What to them are ACIS, AIOB or AMIED—or even CGLI? I know we tend to let our love of qualifications and initials go to our heads in FE. Perhaps we are over-compensating for lack of recognition, or love, or understanding. I must admit I sometimes feel a slight pang of unworthiness when I look at prospectuses and see engineers with three whole lines of letters after their names. I used to wonder if they made them up, except that some of these initials are so peculiar no one would think of inventing them. These letters may not mean much to some people, and they are almost incomprehensible to the non-specialist, but they do have a value.

If you are a building employer it is reassuring to know that the plumbing lecturer at the local college teaching your apprentice is as highly qualified as a plumber can be. Similarly if you are a young man bent on a career in engineering, it is comforting for you and your employer who is sponsoring your sandwich HND to know that you are in the company of first-rate, experienced production engineers. So these strings of initials are not quite as superfluous as they seem. It is true that many of the teachers in further education neither have, nor pretend to have, orthodox academic backgrounds. This, however, is counter-balanced by their specialist technical knowledge and education and the skills acquired through years of practical experience.

We also recruit many of our staff from the secondary schools to teach the academic subjects which are now playing such a prominent part in our work. These teachers are usually attracted to us by the prospect of teaching older students, the opportunities for promotion, or simply by the superior working conditions most colleges offer. It would also be fair to say that a number of teachers, disenchanted with conditions in many urban comprehensives, are finding working in colleges of FE more satisfying professionally. We are fortunate in having very few student problems. Our full-time students are volunteers and well-motivated. While the same cannot be said for all our day-release students, at least we have a variety of effective sanctions for those few who are disruptive or idle.

So our teachers are drawn from a kaleidoscope of occupations and bring with them a vast amount of experience and knowledge which is at the disposal of their students. Some of them have come up the hard way and have often acquired their qualifications through years of part-time study as technical college students.

Thus college staff have an intimate knowledge of the kind of world, be it industrial or commercial, in which their students are working or which they are preparing to enter. They know the difficulties of junior management, the perils of the typing pool, the problems of the shop floor and they are able (or should be!) to illustrate their teaching with vivid and telling examples from life—which the students are quick to recognise as valid.

Students are much quicker on the uptake than we give them credit for and they know that staff with this kind of background are not telling them something they have learned from a book. Their knowledge has been acquired in the hard school of experience. Billy Graham writes how teenagers ask him to 'tell it like it is'—this, staff in further education are uniquely fitted to do.

It leads to a rather special relationship between teacher and student. I see this in action when I go through my engineering workshops where first year apprentices are learning the basic skills of fitting and machining from a group of engineering teachers with a wealth of shop-floor experience. It is a popular picture on college prospectuses and FE publications. The apprentice (note the goggles, cap and protective clothing) crouches over his job held in the lathe-chuck, while the lecturer (clean, white coat) stands beside him, patient, helpful, understanding. And it's true! It happens all the time.

And you find this relationship throughout all departments of the college not just in engineering. I won't for a moment claim that this is necessarily closer than the relationship between the skilled and dedicated teacher in the school and his pupil. It is simply different; a relationship that is based on an esteem and trust springing from a shared experience. It may be experience of the drawing office or building site, but it could equally well be that of the fashion design studio or research lab. I think it is in the handling of this age group with its special problems that teachers in FE have made their distinctive contribution.

One criticism constantly levelled at FE teachers is that they are not 'qualified'; in other words they are not trained teachers. This is fair criticism and must be faced. At present there are some 60,000 full-time teachers in FE of whom more than a third are trained. This is a much higher percentage than a few years ago but it is still unsatisfactory. At least it is a charge that we have recognised and are doing our best to put right.

A few of our untrained lecturers are superb natural teachers but this gift is given to very few of us—and not to nearly so many as untrained teachers think. I must nail my colours to the mast here and say that I believe whole-heartedly in compulsory teacher training. Many teachers entering further education are unaccustomed to the academic life and have unorthodox educational histories. Although they have a sound knowledge of subject matter they all require help in teaching method and educational theory. Teaching is really not as simple as it looks. Professional training makes indifferent teachers passable teachers, average teachers good teachers, and it makes above average teachers very fine teachers indeed. Training is the one simple way in which we in FE can increase our effectiveness as teachers, burnish our image, and earn the plaudits of our colleagues. It will also strengthen our claim for recognition as professional men and women. I find it difficult to reconcile strident claims for professional recognition with a marked lack of enthusiasm for professional training.

It is a pity that many of the older teachers in technical colleges, who teach by the light of nature, have been somewhat lukewarm to this idea. It is no good trying to hide this fact and it has done our reputation some disservice. Fortunately, many have begun to realise the desirability of training and of gaining a teaching certificate, particularly now there is a small financial inducement attached to it.

How in fact do teachers in FE receive teacher training if most of them are recruited direct from industry and commerce? There are two main methods and both revolve round the four colleges of education (technical) at Bolton, Wolverhampton, Huddersfield*, and London (Garnett College). The purpose of these colleges is to train men and women for

---

* This has recently become part of the Faculty of Education of Huddersfield Polytechnic.

teaching posts in the field of FE and all four have expanded considerably during the last few years to meet the need for technical teachers. 'Technical' here includes teachers in such areas as business studies, catering, nursing, office arts, and general studies, as well as those we normally associate with the term.

The entry requirements (and these are broadly applicable to all fields) demand a degree or degree equivalent, a higher national diploma or certificate, or a full technological certificate of the City and Guilds of London Institute. The minimum age of entry is usually 25.

There are numerous men and women who decide to make teaching their career and take the standard one-year full-time course before entering the profession. This is known as a pre-service course and often entails considerable financial sacrifice on their part. Some will have held well paid posts at junior and middle management level before deciding to go into teaching, and many men in the 25–35 age range, whatever their occupations, are married with small children and a large mortgage. They receive a grant, but this, like most grants, is barely adequate and for many quite inadequate.

Thus there is now a tendency to obtain a teaching post first and seek training afterwards, since staff can be sent to colleges of education (technical) on full pay by their local authority. Professional training is normally offered as a four-term sandwich course or as a two-year day-release course plus short periods of full-time attendance. This in-service training is also available of course for teachers who have already been working for some years in further education and more and more are taking advantage of this opportunity as the desirability of becoming trained sinks in.

The aim of these courses is not so much to enlarge the teacher's knowledge of his own subject but to provide full professional training. This has four main sections. First, there is the study of the principles of education with lectures on the aims, structure and organisation of education—with special reference to FE. Next, students study curriculum development and teaching methods which include the techniques and methods relating to their own subject. There is also a course in English designed to improve their powers of communication, both oral and written. Finally there are the periods of teaching practice.

In 1975, national conditions of service were agreed for teachers in FE, and LEAs have since been engaged in the delicate task of implementing them. In general, teachers in FE work a thirty-hour week on a ten-session basis for thirty-eight weeks per year. A session can mean either a morning, an afternoon or an evening, though no member of staff is required to work more than two evenings a week as part of his normal timetable. If a teacher takes an evening class, he has a morning or afternoon off as part of his standard timetable.

So if you see your neighbour who teaches biology at the local college digging his garden on a sunny Wednesday morning this will be his morning off in lieu. He may even be looking for specimens! Similarly, if the Chairman of Governors spots one of the engineering staff having a haircut in town, this man has probably been teaching until 9 or 9.30 p.m. the night before.

Although the normal working week is thirty hours, this does not mean that every lecturer teaches for thirty hours. The amount of time he actually teaches is determined by his grade. This grade reflects the level of work he is handling. The higher the level of work he teaches, the higher his grade; and the higher his grade, the less actual teaching he does. It is left to the LEA and the teachers' organisations to negotiate the number of hours each grade will actually teach. A typical pattern would be as follows:

Lecturers Grade I	..	20 hours per week.
Lecturers Grade II	..	18 hours per week.
Senior Lecturers	..	15 hours per week.
Principal Lecturers	..	13 hours per week.

The balance of time is spent in marking, preparation, visits to employers, research, administration, and other duties as required by the head of department. If a teacher, as frequently happens, is needed to teach for longer hours than this, then he is paid for 'additional duty' or 'overtime' at the part-time teaching rate. Many of us dislike this idea of overtime. It sorts ill with professional status and reflects a little too keenly the background from which a number of our staff have been recruited. However, in the conditions under which we work, when over-large classes have to be split at short notice in September and when sudden demands arise for new courses during the session and calls have to be made upon staff, it is perhaps inevitable. But do not let us pretend that we like it.

In discussing staff, I must not forget to make honourable mention of the part-time staff who play such a significant part in our work. They have been a feature of the colleges since the very earliest days. The full-time staff bear the main burden of the day and evening work, but additional help is always required in the evenings and often during the day. Again, many courses require lecturers with special skills and experience which the full-time staff do not possess. These tend to be people actively concerned in new developments in specialist fields. Examples which spring readily to mind are computer work, management, biochemistry, and specialist aspects of marketing and telecommunications. Add to this the teachers required in the evenings for non-vocational and recreational classes and the total of part-time staff employed by a large college may number anything between 150 and 600. With their breadth of knowledge, skill and experience, they add an extra spice to an already highly seasoned college pudding.

For many years part-time evening class teaching was an accepted avenue of recruitment to the profession. Many engineering and building teachers started their careers in further education by teaching maths or science or workshop technology one or two evenings a week at the local tech. Their work was known to the head of department and when a suitable vacancy occurred among the full-time staff, they stood an excellent chance of being chosen to fill it. Since so much of our vocational work is now done in the day, there are not the opportunities there were for evening teaching. But where it still exists it does provide for some men and women who are thinking of entering the profession a fairly painless way of finding out if they are cut out for teaching.

The hectic expansion of our high noon and, in the last decade, changing syllabuses, fresh methods of examining, new teaching techniques and the demands of industrial training boards, and now the re-thinking required by TEC and BEC, all these have meant increasing calls upon teachers in the colleges. The pace has put our senior staff under considerable strain but all teachers are feeling the pressures. Courses, curricula and examinations alter their form annually: we are given little warning and less time to prepare. On! on! on! they cry and we plunge desperately forward trusting that movement implies improvement. The teachers, faced by the bewildering changes coming at them from all directions, are longing to reach a plateau where they can pause for breath, take stock and consolidate. They all want a chance to see what sort of a wood their trees are making. But I am afraid they aren't going to get it.

The implications for staff of the changes I have mentioned are both obvious and far-reaching. There is the need for technical teachers to keep up-to-date with their subject and this is not always easy with increasing specialisation and fragmentation in the sciences. Teachers of general subjects have to keep themselves informed of developments in the curricula of secondary schools and changes in teaching methods there. For all teachers, regardless of subject, the situation demands a marked flexibility of outlook. It means being receptive to new ideas and techniques plus a willingness to accept change—even if this means scrapping or modifying courses recently established but made obsolete by advances in technology or by shifts in the economic climate. There is a need to assess the direction and quality of our teaching and to turn our attention to such matters as curriculum development (i.e. what to teach, how to teach it, and how to check it has been learnt), and to such pressing problems as professional training, and staff development.

It is all very well for me to carry on in this vein but technical teachers are conservative in their attitudes and their methods. They are understandably reluctant to jettison tried and trusted methods for something which smacks of the new gimmickry. This means we avoid the higher idiocies such as mixed-ability groups, but risk missing something of real value. A nice discrimination is admirable, but I hope that many will look again at their methods in the light of all that is happening around them.

Technical college teaching in the past has suffered from being extremely pedestrian and uninspired with an unhealthy reliance upon notes. There was a tendency for the teacher to lecture rather than teach. In other words he stood (or sat) in front of the class and gave forth endlessly to a captive audience. In extreme cases he read straight out of the textbook. There was no class participation; the students sat there, mute, letting it wash all over them. The only class activity, the only break in the monotony or monologue, was a vast amount of note-taking. The teacher, feeling secure as soon as he turned to the blackboard with the reassuring touch of chalk in his hand, wrote up reams of stuff which was faithfully copied by the students into their exercise books. The students were rather like mediaeval monks copying a textbook—a chapter every Tuesday night. But how illuminating were these manuscripts, one wonders. This explains the faded FE gibe about the notes of the teacher becoming the notes of the student without passing through the mind of either.

This inglorious state of affairs has largely disappeared although, as in other sectors of education, there is still far too much dull and unimaginative teaching about for comfort. This charge applies to all levels of teaching but it is most apparent at the lower end. Perhaps it is rather unfair to blame men teaching craft subjects for lack of imagination and flair in the presentation of their material. But it is a pity there is sometimes a failing to illustrate subject matter by reference to their own practical experience. After all, it is because of this that such men find themselves in the classroom at all. There is a similar failure to capitalise on the often quite extensive practical experience of the students. How much more lively and stimulating for the class if the teacher can relate his lesson to practical situations experienced by himself and his students.

The habit of giving lengthy written notes, sometimes neatly disguised as handouts, dies hard with some, and tends to obscure the virtues of handouts themselves. There is also a little too much of the teacher merely telling, rather than creating situations (where this is appropriate) in which the student is able to discover and learn for himself. I know this, like projects and investigations, is time-consuming and hard work, and therefore unpopular. It is so much simpler just to tell and it makes for a quiet life, but this is not effective teaching.

Like primary and secondary education, FE has a body of teachers who range from the brilliant to the ineffective. The great majority do a sound and unspectacular job in the middle register. What I should like to see on a grand scale is our mastery of subject matter and our practical experience reinforced by more imaginative and effective teaching methods. We should then become a formidable force indeed and the quality of our teaching would be hard to match.

The four colleges of education (technical) have done much during the post-war years to raise the general standard of teaching in FE, not only through courses of professional training but by all manner of short courses. The latter are designed to improve teaching methods in specific subjects, for example shorthand and engineering drawing, and also to introduce staff to new techniques, such as team-teaching and the use of audio-visual aids.

There has been much emphasis in recent years on what is fashionably called 'educational technology'. This appalling title includes closed-circuit television (CCTV), audio-visual aids of all descriptions, programmed texts, and teaching machines. Of these, the first two have come to stay, although CCTV is expensive and little developed, but the third and fourth have made virtually no impact. You don't believe me? In an extensive tour of the United States in 1968 I saw hardly any programmed texts being used and only one teaching machine in action—and this was in the equivalent of a TSA Skills Centre. After a lengthy evaluation period, many Americans feel the claims made for these machines have not been substantiated. Some manufacturers have made a fat profit but their machines are gathering dust in countless cupboards.

I think the most worthwhile contribution to teaching method has been the substantial investment made by colleges in audio-visual aids. The now widespread use of overhead projectors, for example, has markedly improved classroom effectiveness and has proved especially valuable in teaching craft and technician courses. Yet we still have a long way to go before the power and flexibility inherent in television, tapes and other aids is properly harnessed and imaginatively exploited.

I mentioned staff development a little while back and you may have been puzzled by the expression. This idea, which originated in industry and has been taken over and adapted by us, has taken firm root in FE over the last few years. As it spreads slowly through the colleges it is going to prove a most significant influence upon all members of staff.

Staff development can be defined as identifying the professional needs of individual teachers and devising programmes to meet those needs. It has four main aims: to improve current performance and remedy existing weaknesses; to prepare staff for changing duties and responsibilities, and to encourage them to use new methods and techniques in their present posts; to enhance job satisfaction; and to prepare teachers for advancement either in their own college or in the education system generally.

So you can see that staff development is not simply a matter of sending people off on courses, though this is an important part of it. It is primarily an exercise (which takes time and is not easy) in securing the effective use and deployment of that most valuable and expensive part of our resources, the teaching staff. In those colleges where staff development schemes have been established, staff testify to their value.

This leads us naturally to an institution much involved in staff development. FE is fortunate in being the first branch of the educational service to have its own staff college. The idea originally sprung from the Willis Jackson Committee set up by the Ministry of Education in 1957 on the supply and training of teachers in technical colleges. Coombe Lodge, a suitably stately home, was acquired and, after adaptation, was formally opened as a residential staff college in 1963. It had three principal objectives. First, to foster the personal development of the senior staff of further education (i.e. principals and heads of department) and thus improve the management of colleges. Secondly, to enhance the effectiveness of both education and training in all sectors of further education. Its aim was thus 'to identify and study major problems connected with the aims, ideas, and growth of technical education with a view to stimulating new methods and attitudes in the colleges.' Above all, it set out to make itself the national focus for FE, a centre for the exchange and development of ideas between FE and the universities, industry, the professions, and government.

Coombe Lodge stands on a bluff overlooking Blagdon Lake in the valley of the River Yeo, some thirteen miles south-west of Bristol. The valley is thickly wooded and beyond the house the Mendips rise steeply to nearly a thousand feet. At first sight it looks like an Elizabethan mansion, but in fact it was custom-built for a member of the Wills family in the 1930s. The house stands in its own grounds with acres of lawns and sessions are held outside whenever the monsoon allows. It also boasts a croquet lawn which lends a saving Edwardian grace to the prevailing technical chat.

The permanent staff consists of a director, a deputy director cum director of studies, and several staff tutors, and is supplemented by visiting lecturers and course tutors. The college commands a range of visiting speakers of the highest calibre and has a host of contacts in various corridors of power.

I think the staff college's greatest success so far has been in providing management training for senior staff in what have become rather unwieldy and complicated organisations. It quickly put its finger on what was urgently needed, and courses for principals, vice-principals, heads of departments, and young hopefuls have already done much to improve the standard of college management. The staff college also organises courses, usually lasting a week, on some of the outstanding issues in FE. Recent courses have been on such subjects as art and design education, the financing of FE, libraries and resource centres, guidance and counselling, the management of change, and the relations between school and college. Every encouragement is given to those in industry and educational administration to join in and certain conferences are arranged specially for them.

The staff college is already recognised as a major influence on FE in general and on staff development in particular.

Career opportunities for girls

Kissing don't last: cookery do.
The Ordeal of Richard Feverel George Meredith

Girls deserve a chapter to themselves. For many years, careers education for girls has been one of my more attractive professional interests. I was one of their early champions in FE, so I speak here from the heart.

Recent legislation has served to underline the changes that are taking place in the world of work. Although traditional attitudes to employment, both masculine and feminine, will take a long time to change, and although the division of employment into what is appropriate for women and what is appropriate for men will largely continue, the lines of demarcation between men's work and women's work are becoming less marked. There are small but significant numbers of girls now entering engineering and building just as more young men are becoming nurses and secretaries. There will be no large-scale reversal of roles but there will be an increasing range of opportunities for girls in what have hitherto been exclusively male preserves. So we look forward to more girls entering FE and joining traditionally male career courses.

Of course, considerable opportunities already exist. The last twenty years have seen a striking development in the range of full-time vocational courses for girls. Colleges in the last decade have also suddenly become socially acceptable and doubting mothers now trust their doe-eyed daughters to us.

Yet despite momentous post-war changes, the college of FE is still very much a man's world. When our modern colleges were designed the college population was predominantly male. Thus the buildings were designed by men for men, and it is a rare college that is provided with adequate women's common rooms, rest rooms and quiet rooms. This is sad yet hardly surprising since it reflects the ineffable masculine view of an infinite masculine future. Even so it might have occurred to the most misogynistic principal or chief education officer that the time was coming when a monstrous regiment of women would come marching in to redress the balance. New career opportunities for women were rapidly evolving and vocational courses for them were bound to follow. In any case it was hardly as if there were no girls at all in the colleges during the early 1950s. Still, now that young women form an important part of the FE scene (and scenery), their special needs as students should be reflected in our buildings.

This chapter is called 'Career opportunities for girls', and by this I mean those opportunities available through our full-time and part-time courses. I am not talking about girls of degree calibre or the thousands who leave school at 16 every year to become semi-skilled process workers in industry or to supply the lower levels of the retail and distributive trades. I mean girls of average or above average ability. All girls in this ability range can look forward to a worthwhile and satisfying career through further education.

It is the accepted pattern today for young women to continue working after marriage, and for many of them to return to work, full or part-time, when their children start school. Some can hardly wait that long, so strong is the attraction of interesting work among friends compared with the dubious solo delights of housework and cooking. So the relevance of education and training which will prepare them for satisfying careers to which they can return after the marriage/family intermission is pretty obvious.

But it was not always thus, and it is interesting to see the changes in social attitudes to the employment of young women of this type during the last sixty years.

From the turn of the century there were three types of employment open to 'good' girls: office work, teaching, and nursing. This was still the position between the two world wars even though women had demonstrated during the 1914 –18 war their competence and effectiveness in all manner of

E

situations. At the end of the Great War they received the
vote and with it, so they thought, recognition of the important and responsible role women could be called upon to play
in society. But the castle of male dominance was not to be
stormed so easily.

During the 1920s and 1930s, able young women were
underpaid, overworked, overlooked and undervalued. Office
work attracted large numbers and they obtained secretarial
training either through private commercial colleges or by
attending evening classes. The work they did tended to be
low-grade and ill-paid and offered few chances of promotion.
They made no visible impact on management, either at
middle or junior level. Even when they proved capable of
holding down responsible posts, there was great reluctance
to promote them further.

These young women had to contend with deep-seated
masculine prejudices. The arguments are familiar: training
women is basically a waste of time and effort since their
useful working life is short; women are unreliable, incon-
sistent, and emotional, unable to carry responsibility or to
inspire confidence. All this smacks of the nineteenth century
view that women could only be employed in simple repetitive
tasks which exercised their nimble little fingers without tax-
ing their bird-like brains. Sweet shops or sweat shops were
all they could aspire to. And the depression of the 1930s did
little to improve the prospects of women in employment.

Between the wars, both teaching and nursing were ill paid
and barred to the married woman. Women teachers, though
undoubtedly genteel, were a depressed caste. Nursing, despite bad pay, poor working conditions, and unimaginative
discipline was able to attract thousands of intelligent girls
with a strong sense of service and much latent idealism. After
all, if she did not want to teach or go into secretarial work
what else could a bright girl do?

What is the position now thirty years after a second world
war? There are two major achievements to report, the introduction of equal pay, and the establishment of the Equal
Opportunities Commission. And what else has changed?

In the secretarial world, working conditions and pay have

become steadily more attractive. The private executive secretary and PA (personal assistant) have a glamorous, trendy image and are much used and wooed by subtle advertisers. There is a clear career ladder rising from junior to shorthand-typist through secretary and private secretary to personal assistant. Skilled and experienced secretaries are like manna in the desert and command fearsome salaries, especially in London. Sharing a flat with several friends, male and female, the secretary-bird is the envy of her contemporaries.

How do girls start? In the last chapter I mentioned the secretarial courses available in the business studies department. These courses are designed to cater for both the outright beginners and those who have learned some typewriting and perhaps a little shorthand at school. Most colleges offer one- and two-year secretarial courses for school leavers. These courses not only give a thorough grounding in what are called nowadays the 'office arts' (shorthand, typewriting and office practice) but also continue the student's general education, usually with a chance of taking certain subjects at O level. Increasing emphasis is being laid upon training in a model office where girls are introduced, often by a series of related projects, to the latest business machines and office procedures.

Those girls whose English is of a suitable standard learn audio-typewriting which is becoming very common in the larger offices. There are various audio-systems but the basic principle is that the executive, instead of calling in his secretary and giving her a letter which she takes down in shorthand in her notebook and later transcribes on the typewriter, dictates letters, memos, reports, etc. into some form of recording device. Then all the audio-typist has to do is to play the recording back via head-phones and transcribe it directly onto the typewriter. The saving is obvious.

Many girls, trained as shorthand-typists, are often disappointed when they go into business and find themselves employed virtually as copy-typists under the audio-system. Gone is the personal contact and the chance for tea and sympathy. They see themselves as business battery hens, with the emphasis on output and few excuses for leaving their

cages. Girls brooding over their future can console themselves with the thought that while there are still so many
small offices, there will always be a steady demand for the
competent shorthand-typist.

There seems to be a growing demand for copy-typists so
most colleges run one-year courses for girls who find shorthand hard but will make effective copy-typists or junior
clerks. At the other end of the scale there are secretarial
courses for girls coming in at 18 with one or two A levels.
These girls are potential PAs and in an intensive year's
course they may combine secretarial subjects with foreign
languages. Girls of this calibre can often obtain good posts
in firms with a flourishing export trade or find well-paid and
attractive jobs in Europe.

The hospitals have realised there are too many careers
open nowadays to the type of girl upon whom they used to
rely and they have been finding it difficult to recruit enough
potential SRNs (State Registered Nurses) even with the
present low entry qualifications. Although matrons would
dearly love to obtain student nurses aged 18-plus with several
A levels, they have to set their sights rather lower, although
there is some evidence that this picture is changing dramatically in some parts of the country.

Many colleges offer full-time pre-nursing courses of one-
or two-years for girls who are temperamentally suitable for
nursing and capable of gaining the necessary GCE O and A
level passes for entry into training.

There is also a part-time route called the cadet scheme for
those who do not wish to stay on at school or college but are
eager to get into hospital work. A girl applies to the matron
of a hospital which takes cadets, and if accepted, becomes an
employee receiving a small salary. She attends college on
two days a week and spends the rest of the week working on
carefully regulated duties in the hospital. Then at the end of a
year's course she enters full-time training. This is a very
effective bridge between school and hospital life and for
many hospitals it is the only way they can guarantee an
adequate intake of student nurses into their preliminary
training schools. Cadet schemes are not cheap to operate

but when hospitals, like many in the north-west, depend on them for two-thirds of their student nurse intake, they become a necessary investment.

So far we have been talking about girls who are potential SRNs, those who will become the skilled technicians and junior managers of the future. But there is still plenty of scope for the girl who cannot satisfy the entry requirements to SRN training. She can become an SEN or State Enrolled Nurse. These are essentially bedside nurses performing practical nursing functions under the supervision of a ward sister or staff nurse. Some hospitals offer SEN cadetships and there are many SENs who have done well, acquired extra qualifications, and gone on to SRN training.

In passing, I should stress that the National Health Service offers a variety of interesting careers to girls. Besides the specialised nursing courses I have just mentioned, there are also opportunities in administration and housekeeping.

Teaching remains a popular and satisfying career for a woman and teachers now receive professional salaries. To be considered for training by a college a girl requires a minimum of five O levels. But this is a bare minimum and most girls nowadays will need to have one or more A levels to get a place. Normally these are obtained at school but some girls prefer to transfer at 16 to a college of FE to take additional O and A levels.

With the cut-back in teacher recruitment, many girls who would normally have entered colleges of education will look to FE in future for further and higher education.

So much for the traditional pastures. If the position here is one of modified rapture, there is encouraging news from other fields. During the last twenty years the range of career opportunities for young women has widened considerably. Hairdressing, nursery nursing, demonstrating, fashion, social work, institutional management, art and design, are examples of careers which are now backed up by full-time courses in the colleges. Most of these are available in your area but certain courses, such as those for the clothing industry, for example, will only be available at a few colleges like the London College of Fashion or the Hollings College in Manchester.

There has also been a development of career prospects in what are somewhat chillingly described as fields ancillary or supplementary to medicine. Girls with the necessary O and A levels can train as dietitians, occupational therapists, orthoptists, physiotherapists, radiographers, dental auxiliaries, chiropodists, and remedial gymnasts. Courses suitable for some of these posts exist in FE. An encouraging thing about these careers is that the financial rewards, once so niggardly considering the lengthy training involved, are now very much improved.

At a lower level there has been a welcome expansion, as in the United States, of careers as technicians. From the basic laboratory assistant (for whom there is an apparently unending demand from industry, government, and the universities) there have now evolved careers such as dental nurses and medical laboratory technicians, all supported by college courses.

Two other major industries, catering and retailing, have emerged as offering fine prospects for able girls. Catering used to be one of the most unattractive and least rewarding of industries and few other industries paid so little attention to training. This has been drastically altered by the pressure of the Industrial Training Act and by the industry itself. Catering has made great strides in putting its house in order and is now very training conscious. Many colleges up and down the country have hotel and catering departments offering the new pattern of courses which provides a splendid start in the industry. Besides courses which give girls a sound knowledge of professional cookery and food service, there are courses for book-keeper receptionists as well as fine opportunities for those girls aiming at supervisory posts in the industry. The finished products are in great demand and college staff, because of their connections, are often able to place students advantageously.

Retailing has also suffered from an unhappy history. This, like factory work, has always been one of the main destinations for early school leavers and the less able girl. Retailing to most people means selling things in shops. What few parents realise are the opportunities which exist at the higher levels, particularly in those companies which run chains of shops known as the 'multiples'. These are of three main types: supermarkets, large stores, and those shops which sell one type of goods such as food, or shoes, or men's clothing. These multiples, like Marks and Spencer, Jaeger and Dolcis, are enterprising and progressive organisations with training schemes to support their merchandising policies. Such firms need buyers, personnel officers, cashiers, department manageresses, executives, and these are responsible and well-paid posts.

Although girls can go straight into multiple retailing at 16, I must stress here the value of taking the ordinary national diploma in business studies. I have mentioned this in an earlier chapter, but it can bear repeating. This is an ideal course for girls aiming at executive positions in business. If they wish, girls can also combine the diploma course with secretarial training and this makes a very effective preparation for the business world.

Let me hasten to say that this chapter does not seek to provide a careers directory for girls—just in case you thought I was about to do so. I have simply tried to underline the quite remarkable range of career courses open to girls of average and above average ability via the college of FE. Although I have been speaking so far mainly in terms of full-time courses, I should point out that for many of the careers I have mentioned there are part-time courses available. In other words, a girl can secure a job first and then obtain further education and training on a part-time basis.

A word of caution here. Day-release, as we have seen, is the peculiarly British response to furthering the education and training of young workers in engineering and building. Not unnaturally, it has never found much favour with those industries where women form the majority of the labour force. It has never found much favour either in the banking, insurance and commercial sectors. All the Votes-for-Women chaps like myself hoped that day-release for young women would be stimulated by the 1964 Henniker-Heaton Report. (Whatever happened to that?) In fact the number receiving day-release in commerce has decreased in the last few years and continues to do so. It is a dismal picture and one that the activities of the various training boards have so far done disappointingly little to correct.

Girls thinking in terms of a specific career will naturally rely upon the advice given by the specialists in the careers service and by the careers teachers in the schools. But I feel they would be well-advised to take a full-time college course, where appropriate, rather than rely upon part-time courses for their future education and training. If a girl does decide to go straight into a job, then she and her parents would do well to ensure it is one in which she will be encouraged to attend the local college on day-realease.

Let me end this chapter by making two points about the education and training of young women. All of us, except die-hard anti-feminists, want women to make their proper contribution to society. We have seen that most girls today can look forward to a career, a course of training followed by satisfying employment, to which they can return after having children. For many young women whose horizons lie far beyond the bottom of their gardens, bringing up children and managing a home, although a valuable and honourable occupation, is no longer an adequate fulfilment. It is important for them and for society that their ambitions find expression in careers.

I want young women encouraged to realise their potential and to lead full and satisfying lives. I am sorry if this sounds like some politician advocating the opening-up of underdeveloped countries. We have all had cases like the girl with eight O levels who applies for a hairdressing course. She has every right to do so, but I hope she is urged to set her sights a little higher. Sadly, many girls seem only too happy to accept posts well below their true level of ability.

This brings me to my second point, which is economic. When the country finds itself from time to time in serious financial difficulties, this pool of ability, our young women, represents about the last of our untapped resources. Can we afford this loss of potential any longer? Can we merrily carry on ignoring the contribution that such young women can make, with suitable prompting and prodding, to the economy?

It is no good claiming the difficulties are too great. The barriers are nothing like so formidable as they once were. The door of opportunity is ajar and there are all kinds of inviting prospects beyond. All a girl has to do is give the door a gentle push and pass through.

CHAPTER SEVEN

Behind the scenes

For I also am a man set under authority, having under me
soldiers; and I say unto one, Go and he goeth;
and to another, Come, and he cometh; and to my servant
Do this, and he doeth it.

St Luke 7: 8

A college of FE today is a large complex organisation.
How large and complex you probably do not realise. It may
well represent a capital investment in buildings and equipment of between one million and four million pounds. The
full-time teaching staff may number anything from one
hundred to three hundred, with an annual salary bill of over
one and a half million pounds.

Again, there is the army of part-time staff, day and
evening, who tend to be numbered in hundreds rather than
in tens. Add to this the numerous non-teaching staff, such
as the college office staff, caretakers, cleaners, refectory staff,
maintenance men, laboratory and workshop technicians,
storekeepers, library staff and you have a sizeable community! And all this costs a great deal of your money to run.

How are colleges governed, organised and managed? All
colleges have governing bodies whose composition is determined by what is called an Instrument of Government and
whose powers are laid down in the Articles of Government.
In their early days and during the great post-war expansion,
many colleges had governing bodies established much on the
lines of those for secondary schools. There was a prepon-
derance, you might almost say a totality, of elected members
(i.e. local councillors and aldermen) plus a few co-opted
members. Colleges grew very rapidly but there was limited
opportunity for men from industry and commerce to serve
on the governing bodies. Yet the colleges' *raison d'être* was
to serve the needs of this huge sector of the economy; the

colleges had long-established links with it and depended on it for their students. It is true that among elected members there were occasionally representatives of local business and of the trade unions, but they tended to be in a minority, particularly the former.

It was only natural, I suppose, that the elected members and the officers in many local authorities should want to keep a pretty tight grip on these burgeoning institutions. Some were rather put out that the new colleges, which had developed almost overnight from lusty infants into hulking giants, refused to be treated as primary schools and wanted a much greater measure of independence.

The DES was sympathetic towards the colleges and it determined that governing bodies should be more broadly based and have more power. It also decreed that there should be staff participation in the government of colleges and in the conduct of academic matters. In 1970 it recommended that governing bodies should be between twenty and twenty-five strong and that roughly one-third should be LEA members. Direct representation from industry and commerce, including both management and unions, should form another third. The remaining places should be filled by representatives of relevant professions, by representatives of LEAs contributing a significant number of students and, above all, by representatives of the staff and students. Thus, it hoped, would LEA control be reduced and the independence of governing bodies enhanced.

Staff representation is now widespread, with the governing body usually including two or three members of the full-time staff, in addition to the principal as an ex-officio governor. Governors and principals are either attuned or resigned to this development and both feel the best policy is to come to terms with the situation gracefully.

Many colleges also have representatives of the students as governors. It is fair to say that although student governors generally play a somewhat muted rule in discussion, governors have been surprised by their articulate and sensible contributions when matters connected with their special interest crop up.

The governing body normally meets once a term. The public has the impression that the governors determine the policy of the college but this is not really the case. Policy in further education stems in fact from more than one source. Much of it is made nationally by the DES and local authorities can do little but implement the tablets handed down to them. Policy can occasionally come from the education committee of the LEA, especially when that committee happens to contain a vigorous educationist in his or her own right. More frequently at local authority level, it emanates from a strong-willed director of education and his officers and is endorsed by the education committee. It can also come, and often does, from the principal and/or the academic board. What the governing body does in fact is to comment on, endorse, amend or disfigure proposals laid before it by the principal or the director of education. But no matter where it comes from, the governors normally look to the professionals, the principal and the director of education, for advice and guidance on the many issues affecting an expanding, changing and complex organisation.

I mentioned that the objectives of the DES were staff participation in government and more effective staff involvement in the conduct of academic matters. It was hoped to achieve the latter through the establishment of academic boards and these were set up at the same time as the new governing bodies. All colleges now have academic boards (at varying stages of development) and they are proving one of the most important internal happenings of recent years. A typical academic board consists of the principal (who acts as chairman), vice-principal, registrar, heads of department, librarian, and a number of the teaching staff.

Boards vary in their powers and some have tended to assume wider responsibilities because it has been found difficult and undesirable in practice to define and deal with academic affairs in isolation. Matters such as finance, building, staffing and administration all bear inescapably upon discussions about the academic work of an institution.

Like certain other bodies, the academic boards tend to spawn committees. If we are sometimes a little cynical about professional committee men and those teachers who prefer a long talk to a short class, at least the committees have the virtue of providing real involvement for a fair number of staff in decisions affecting the running and development of the college. They have certainly clipped the wings of the tyrant-principal and the power-crazed head of department and brought a new cohesion and consensus to the management of our colleges. There is no going back now. College life would be infinitely poorer without the activities of the academic board.

The actual day-to-day management of the college is usually conducted by the principal and vice-principal supported by regular meetings with the registrar and heads of department. This committee is popularly known as the 'heads committee' and is regarded in many colleges as the real centre of power. At these meetings all kinds of topics affecting the conduct, welfare and future of the college are discussed. Matters range from the gay to the solemn, and there is inevitably a great deal of administrative detail. I like to think, however, it is important detail and discussion helps to make the administrative machine function smoothly and efficiently. One of the purposes of these meetings is to discuss the ideas and reactions of members of staff for, if the word goes down, it is equally important to let it come up. Regular meetings enable the principal and his colleagues to form conclusions and take decisions from a broad band of experience and give them an opportunity to deal swiftly with sensitive matters which if left unattended may fester and cause trouble.

Above all, the heads of department and the registrar feel that with the principal and vice-principal they form the management team. Their experience is being drawn upon and their wishes and opinions are being consulted and respected. As for the principal, well, no principal, with one or two exceptions, claims to have a monopoly of the divine revelation, and any of his ideas and proposals are all the better for being refined and tempered by exposure to senior colleagues.

The principal is the chief executive, the general manager,

solely responsible to the governors for the management of
the college. He is a lonely man. Not for him the cynicism
and badinage of the staff room; not for him, as for a head
of department, the companionship and solace of the other
heads and his senior colleagues. The principal is both
initiator and executor of policy, accountable for the acts of
his servants who range from the highly conscientious to the
merely irresponsible. He is the captain of a ship, with
officers of uneven quality, a large and motley crew who
move him from pride to desperation, and a tremendous
passenger list of varying origins and destinations. He tries
to steer a consistent course through the stormy seas of
education, buffeted by the demands of the DES on one side
and the local authority on the other, and always in danger
of being pooped by his governors. The winds of change blow
hot and then cold, they veer and back with little warning.
He stands on the bridge trying to see the way ahead,
ignorant of what lies in wait for him below the horizon. His
ship may lack adequate maintenance, it may be grossly overcrowded but somehow he is expected to bring it safely into
harbour at the end of each session.

But the principal does have someone to commune with
and confide in. All medium-sized colleges and above now
have a vice-principal to assist the principal in the management of the college. This is a recognition of the size of the
executive load.

The functions of the vice-principal will naturally vary
according to the whims of his principal. But there seems to
be a recognisable job specification emerging in which the
vice-principal is given responsibility for the day-to-day
running of the establishment together with special responsibilities for such matters as staff development, allocation of
accommodation and, increasingly, financial matters. Some
vice-principals, because of their background or special
expertise, will involve themselves in curriculum development. The main danger to avoid is the vice-principal
becoming a kind of educational Pooh Bah.

I think I should explain at this point that if the basic unit
in a college is the class, then the major organisational device

is the department. This is one of the most enduring traditional features of technical college organisation. It has its
drawbacks and its detractors but it has proved a remarkably
effective and flexible instrument over the years. The department is essentially a related group of courses (full-time,
day-release and evening) in one discipline, such as engineering or construction.

The head of department in a college should not be
confused with a head of department in a secondary school.
The latter is a subject head, responsible for the teaching
organisation of his subject throughout the school. Thus a
head of English in a fairly large comprehensive school
would have perhaps eight or nine teachers in his department.
The college head of department is a horse of a very different
colour. It is a difference of kind not degree. He may control
a full-time staff of between ten and fifty, supplemented by
numerous part-time staff, both day and evening. A large
department will often have more staff than a small college—
which gives you an idea of the responsibility a head of
department carries in FE.

In organising his department a head will ensure that the
senior members of his staff have clearly delegated responsibility for certain areas of work. For example in a business
studies department there will probably be a principal
lecturer in charge of management work and in an engineering
department a senior lecturer in charge of all motor vehicle
courses. He will then give responsibility for specific courses
within those areas to various teachers. The assignment of
carefully graduated responsibilities to junior members of his
department is an important part of the head's job, and vital
for effective staff development. He will hold meetings from
time to time to explain new trends in college policy to his
staff and to deal with domestic matters. These will be in
addition to any general staff meetings called by the principal.
Such meetings, by the way, are very hard to arrange in a
large college and can usually only be held at the start and
end of the session. This makes the principal even more
dependent upon his heads for the responsible dissemination
of policy decisions and for their execution.

A head of department is a powerful figure, responsible for an important part of the college's work, given the authority commensurate with it and trusted by his principal to exercise that authority responsibly with the minimum of interference. It is upon the heads of department that all turns in a college and I cannot stress this too strongly. A good principal backed by loyal, able, experienced and well-qualified heads of department means a vigorous progressive college with high academic and social standards. That same principal with only a poor-to-middling bunch of heads will have a difficult task in attempting to raise standards and expand the work of his college.

Remember that a principal inherits his heads of department; he is not able as in industry to hire and fire and to create his own team. And perhaps for everyone's peace of mind, it is just as well. As a principal at Elsinore once commented, 'Use every man after his desert, and who should 'scape whipping?'

Let us look now for a moment at the non-teaching side of the college. The man responsible to the principal for this is called the registrar or senior administrative officer. This is a key post in the college and most registrars are scandalously underpaid and overworked. He is responsible for four main areas in the college, the most important of which is the college office, the heart of the college administration. Here all the myriad clerical procedures involved in running a large organisation take place.

Here the students' records are kept (they are all computerised now), fees collected, examination entries made, and returns for the DES and the LEA prepared. Here all the correspondence from the heads of department and senior staff is dealt with and material duplicated for the teaching staff. This is where the accounts are kept, goods ordered, invoices checked, estimates prepared, and a hundred and one other things done besides. The number of staff in a college office is usually determined by some LEA formula but, formula or not, it is a rare college office that never complains of being understaffed.

The college office is the main contact between the public

and the college. It deals with enquiries from prospective students, receives visitors, enrols students, pacifies the aggrieved and reassures the timid; its telephones are never silent. It is usually the first part of the college with which the public comes into contact and it is important that the impression is favourable. Pleasant, efficient service is the watchword and office staff are selected with care.

As well as the college office, the registrar is responsible for the refectory through a catering officer or manageress who may be controlling a full-time equivalent staff of twenty in a medium sized college, or forty or more in a mammoth institution.

Also responsible to the registrar is the head caretaker, who will have several assistants and numerous full- and part-time cleaners plus, in some cases, attendants and porters. Because colleges are going full blast from 9 a.m. to 9 or 10 p.m. each day and since many engineering and building departments are open for forty-eight weeks of the year, keeping a huge place like a modern college clean is a major task and a major headache. It is not simply a problem of cleaning a few offices or one or two workshops. The head caretaker has to plan the cleaning of a mixture of classrooms, libraries, halls, laboratories, workshops, studios, offices, and gymnasia. This has to be fitted in before the college starts in the mornings, while the classes are in session during the day, in the evenings, or at the weekends.

Our fabric takes a tremendous hammering during the week with the intensive use we give it, and it is difficult to achieve that high degree of cleanliness and sparkle we should dearly like to see.

The fourth area for which the registrar is responsible is maintenance, and this refers to both the fabric and the equipment. All colleges have workshop technicians to maintain the machine tools and equipment in the engineering workshops, and laboratory technicians to maintain apparatus and equipment, set up experiments, and prepare work in laboratories ranging from building science to electronics and from chemical plant operation to biology. Local authorities vary widely in their attitude towards technician provision

F

and it is usually much easier to obtain a teacher than an extra workshop technician. But more and more LEAs are at last realising that it pays to maintain expensive machine tools and specialist plant. Furthermore, if we are to make the most effective use of our skilled teachers, they must have adequate technician support.

So you can see that the registrar's responsibilities are wide-ranging and demanding. They are as exacting as those of any head of department and an able registrar is a boon. Principals recognise this by treating him on a par with the heads of department and ensuring that this is known throughout the college. This is why the registrar attends meetings of heads of department or the academic board as of right.

Each major department of a college has an advisory committee, looked after by the appropriate head of department. These committees consist of people representing local interests and their function is to advise on all aspects of the work and progress of a particular department. For example, the Engineering Advisory Committee will consist of local employers, particularly those supplying large numbers of students to the college, representatives from the trades unions, training officers, and representatives from the relevant Training Boards. It is very convenient if a governor acts as chairman of each advisory committee. This means that, although the functions of these committees are purely advisory, any resolutions or recommendations they make go up to the governing body for consideration with added authority. This is important if you wish to attract influential people from industry and business to serve on your advisory committee. They are not going to be keen on the idea of spending their valuable time making recommendations if these are not going to be seriously treated by the governing body. Advisory committees form a valuable link between the community and the college and give local industry a chance to play a useful part at grass roots level.

There are three other important groups which are normally found in technical colleges: the staff association, the students' union, and the NATFHE* branch. I shall deal

* National Association of Teachers in Further and Higher Education.

with the students' union in another chapter, but I must stress in this context that with the importance students' unions have assumed in colleges, it behoves principals to come to terms with them pretty quickly. Frequent meetings between the students' union committee and the principal create an atmosphere of mutual trust where grievances can be aired, criticisms levelled and answered, and constructive suggestions put forward for discussion. I suppose it is only natural that so often we seem to be dealing with grievances and demands, but this must not be allowed to obscure the contribution such meetings have to the harmonious running of our colleges.

Obviously the degree of independence which the students enjoy depends upon the age range of the student body, but I think most senior staff who have had dealings with student committees recognise the sense of responsibility and fairness which quite young members display.

The staff association is primarily concerned with the promotion of the general welfare of the staff (generously interpreted) and with arranging all kinds of social activities designed to foster a warm glow of togetherness. It tends to be hyper-active at Christmas and then to subside into a kind of lethargy, with occasional spasms at Easter and the end of session.

Incidentally, you learn more about your staff in three hours on the dance floor than in three terms in the college. But that's another story.

I know that in some colleges the staff association gets terribly tangled up with the purely professional interests of staff—which leads to all kinds of unholy rows and complications. That way madness lies. I have always tried to keep the two distinct, because I feel strongly that the promotion of teachers' professional interests should be the province of the teachers' professional organisation. Nearly every college has its NATFHE branch to which many of the staff belong. The branch holds regular meetings and it is with the officers of this body that the principal deals over professional matters. These may range from serious problems to apparently quite minor points about working conditions—but ones which are far from trivial in their impact on morale.

A wise principal will seek to take the officers of both these associations into his confidence and keep them aware of what is happening, and likely to happen, both locally and nationally on matters which may affect the staff. Mutual trust builds up and the staff know that, as in the case of comments and ideas put up via their heads of department, their problems, suggestions and complaints will be dealt with fairly and we hope quickly. They will not always get the answer they want, but at least they will get an answer.

What I have said in these last few pages is an appeal, none the less potent for being implicit, for good communications inside colleges. Though I am not struck with much of the current claptrap about communications, bad lines of communication certainly do a great deal of damage in colleges as in all major organisations. Part of the art of management lies in keeping the channels of communication at all levels not merely unclogged, but positively flowing with a stream of information, decisions and encouragement.

CHAPTER EIGHT

Aspects of student life

I have, all my life long, been lying till noon; yet
I tell all young men, and tell them with great sincerity,
that nobody who does not rise early will ever do any good.

Dr Johnson

Examine me, O Lord, and prove me.

Psalm XXVI

College life is like farming. We share a common satisfying rhythm. First comes the seed-time, next a period for nurture and consolidation, and finally the harvest—with an occasional outbreak of blight to save us from complacency. Like the farmer's year, our session is punctuated by bouts of intense activity and fallow periods of comparative calm.

Intense activity is very much the keynote of early September when the college session opens. A few colleges help new full-time students find their feet by means of induction courses. 'Induction' means a formal introduction to something and such courses, lasting from a day to a week, prepare the new arrival to take his place with confidence in a large organisation. The value of these courses to both college and industry has been stressed in recent years but I think most colleges rely upon the natural adaptability, curiosity and resilience of youth.

Course tutors usually arrange some kind of unofficial induction for their new full-time students. Students are taken round the building, and shown such salient features as the refectory, college office, hall, sports hall, library and head of department's room. The head of department will talk about college and departmental organisation and what he requires from his students.

Sometimes the principal will speak to all new full-time students in the hall. This is one of the rare occasions when students will actually see and hear this remote being. If they do not meet him during their first week, they may never do so during the rest of their course and he will remain a cypher at the bottom of the posters. Part-time students often grumble about having been students for three or four years without having any idea what the principal looks like. Some principals combat this by talking to each new batch of day-release students on their first day of attendance. This means saying much the same thing five times over but at least it ensures that these students know who the principal is and realise he is just as interested in them as in the full-time students—and this appears important to many of them.

The pattern of college life will not be entirely unfamiliar to the full-time student coming in straight from school. The working day is likely to be a little longer (9 a.m. to 4.30 p.m. is typical) but there is usually an hour for lunch plus morning and afternoon breaks.

The working day for the day-release students is not quite so straightforward. In order to cover the syllabus of their courses properly, technician and craft students have to spend about nine hours per week at the college. Assuming the length of the working day is six and a half hours (excluding the lunch hour) then there is another two and a half hours to be fitted in. This can be done either by bringing the students in on another evening or by lengthening their day of attendance. In the latter case the students have a break for tea at 4.30 p.m. and then have what is pleasantly called a 'twilight' period from 5 p.m. onwards.

Educationally, another evening has much to commend it because most students, come half-past four, have pretty well had it. Even the craft apprentice whose work is mainly practical gets a little weary as the sun sinks in the west. Yet most young men would rather have a longer day than come in on another evening. Where the day has to be extended, we save any practical element in the curriculum for the 'twilight' session. The pattern varies from college to college, but we all try to combat the fatigue factor.

One thing that does strike many new students as unfamiliar is the lack of what we might call a home base—a sixth form area, a room of their own. This impression is heightened by the furniture which in most classrooms consists of tables rather than the normal desks with storage space. Students therefore have to keep their books, PE kit, and coats in built-in wooden lockers or in tall metal lockers lining the walls of the corridors. Usually only full-time students have lockers. Day-release students have to hump their books around and, since few colleges have cloakrooms, they have to carry their coats, helmets, gauntlets, scarves, fleecy-lined boots, lamps, pumps, and other removables as well.

Which brings us to dress. Today the keynote is informality and there is no attempt to regulate what students should wear. All we insist on is appropriate protective clothing. Most of our students are too hard up to dress like young stockbrokers or top models and they are casually and sensibly clad. However, art students remain notorious for bizarre gear and there are always individualists who seize the chance to roll up in monks' habits, saris, caftans, football jerseys, and strange hats.

There is no point in a principal getting over-excited about dress and hair. He can take comfort in the thought that fashion today is a fleeting thing and the more audacious it becomes the more ephemeral it is likely to be. Such little vanities brush the colleges lightly and then wing on. Accept that informality is here to stay, and remember that striped socks, beads, wedgies and knitted hats, like other glories, all slowly pass away.

I know long hair on young men arouses a quite unhinging irritation in many of us associating it as we do with dirt, decadence and debility. But this, too, is a passing fancy. What is refreshing is to see the students at a college dance. The young men are smartly turned out in sharp suits (at least they are up here in the old-fashioned north-west) and the girls in their long dresses make a little springtime in the blood. They are a very pleasant crowd indeed.

New arrivals will be reassured to find that classes are not over large. Full-time students will find themselves being taught in classes of between ten and twenty-four. Large classes will be split for practical and laboratory work into more easily supervised groups. In the part-time day technician and craft courses, the number of students a teacher can supervise adequately for practical work tends to control the size of classes. The accepted maximum for practical classes is fifteen, but this is a maximum and there are many occasions when safety or the type of work dictate a smaller number. This rule of fifteen has tended, perhaps not unnaturally, to be applied to non-practical classes as well.

It is inviting disaster to generalise about FE students because the various categories differ in their responses to college life and there are different reactions within the categories themselves. But I must risk one or two sweeping statements at this point. For the sake of clarity, I shall talk in this chapter about our two main types of customer—the full-time and the day-release student.

Despite the varied nature of their backgrounds, full-time students form a fairly homogeneous crowd. Most of them are straight from school, conditioned to academic routine, with standard responses and orthodox attitudes to work. They are all volunteers with strong motivation and they cheerfully co-exist within a familiar frame of routine and minimal regulations—especially if the reasons for the few regulations are explained to them. If you are fair, firm and straightforward with them, treat them as reasonable people listen to their views and criticisms and remedy any genuine grievances quickly, then you are a good way towards establishing an atmosphere in which the educational process can take place.

It is not quite so simple to generalise about the day-release students, predominantly male, mainly from the engineering, building, and manufacturing industries. Certainly the older students realise the importance of their studies in terms of pay, promotion and prospects. They are purposeful and sensible students who provide a counterweight to the swarms of younger apprentices. These 16 and 17 year olds are lively lads indeed, and the compulsory day at college offers one or two temptations to boys in the first flush of employment and adult life.

A few of them are rather reluctant attenders and this shows through in their conduct and their attitude to subjects like

In the public salon girls learn one of the most important skills of their trade—how to deal efficiently and pleasantly with the clients.

Pre-nursing students absorb the theory.

Nursery-nursing students applying the practical.

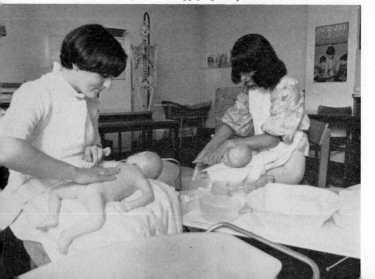

Signing on . . . The Students' Union welcomes new members at the start of the academic year.

The value of physical activity and recreation to the well-being of the students is recognised and catered for.

Courses on computer appreciation and computer languages now play an important part in many business studies departments.

The resources centre introduces students to a new dimension in learning and a new stimulus in their studies. Specialist staff are on call to advise on the use of films, tapes and slides.

English and general studies which seem to them to have no relevance to their job. These subjects, and to a lesser extent science and maths, rouse only unpleasant memories of failure at school—a world they thought they had waved goodbye to for ever.

This tiny minority, and it is tiny, can be a nuisance both inside the classroom and out; it is the price all non-selective establishments pay. This element occasionally delights in fits of wanton damage. Colleges are vulnerable here not simply because rooms and equipment and other facilities are easily accessible but because they consciously set out to treat all students, the feckless and malicious included, as responsible young adults. So they are easy meat for the odd activist and the active odd-ball. Yet if a few of our students are rather difficult to love, even for most of these (if they stay with us) the penny drops about the age of 17 to 18. Dimly they begin to perceive the opportunities the college and their employer are putting before them. It is interesting and rewarding to see them settle down and mature.

A problem which has exercised some staff over the years is that of creating a sense of belonging, a feeling of corporate unity among the full- and part-time students so that they feel part of the college community. It is only natural, perhaps, that our efforts have been concentrated on the full-time students. But it is not easy. Colleges do not have such tools of togetherness as morning assemblies, year meetings, house systems and competitive games. We are organised on a strict departmental basis and the barriers are hard to break down. Our efforts in fact are not very successful. Students, like other groups, are drawn together by community of interest and, if they identify at all, they tend to identify with their department or with a section within a department. It would also be misleading to pretend there is much contact between full-time and part-time students—there is some, but not a great deal.

Accepting these limitations, colleges do try to foster a sense of community and to cut across departmental boundaries by such activities as drama, music, sport, and holidays abroad.

This is all very much standard school and university stuff which young people expect any self-respecting institution to provide or trigger off. I merely draw attention to it here to show that colleges of FE are very much concerned with the need to enrich the quality of college life and provide opportunities for personal development.

Colleges have their problems. Take clubs and societies, for instance, one of the obvious ways through which students can identify. Usually these meet after the full-time classes finish in the afternoon or else meetings are squeezed into the lunch hour. Even at lunch-time it is not easy to get everyone together because most colleges have staggered lunch hours. If the college serves a rural or semi-rural area (and even if it doesn't) there is a mad dash for buses and trains at the end of the day which will not be denied. Furthermore, most students stay with us for only one or two years so that there is little continuity and this partly accounts for the curious spasms which afflict their activities. Student interest is like a yo-yo, up one moment and down the next.

When we turn to part-time students we run into problems because, inevitably, clubs can only exist through the support of full-time students. If a day-release student is interested in a particular club or activity and this happens to meet or take place on a day other than his day of attendance then he is unlucky. Fortunately he can take part in the general social events, like dances and concerts, and in such week-end activities as canoeing, fishing, fell-walking and camping. You will notice the major games are missing. Those day-release students who are keen on soccer and cricket have already developed loyalties to a club or a works side before they come to college.

Staff are concerned that the part-time student who looms so large in their work should not be left out and they do all they can to make him feel part of the scheme of things. If this aim is not always realised, at least the college gives the part-time student a recognisable pattern of educational advancement relevant to his employment in an environment offering many opportunities for personal development. Above all, he is being taught by men and women who take a genuine

interest in his progress and to whom he can turn for dis-
interested advice.

Early in the term students are involved in elections for the
officers and committee of the Students' Union (SU for short).
This committee, representing both full- and part-time students, has an important role and, now more than ever before,
its successful functioning is vital to the well-being of the
college.

It forms the main link between the students and the staff
and governors. It is usual for one of the business studies
department to be senior treasurer and to have a member of
staff who acts as the student liaison officer. These posts are
neither simple to fill nor easy to hold and the men and
women who willingly take on this task are worth their weight
in gold. They create a bond of trust between staff and students
and exert a beneficial influence in the counsels of the SU.

The SU is given (or assumes) as much authority and freedom as possible—some SUs are autonomous—but in those
colleges where most of the students are under 18 there is a
need for father-figures to lurk in the background with words
of caution and advice. The principal meets the SU from time
to time and he is normally immediately available to its officers. He neglects it at his peril.

In many colleges of further education, SU representatives
are now members of the governing body and may also sit on
the academic board and tother internal committees.

Besides its midfield linking role, the SU's main function,
like that of most associations of its kind, is to promote the
interests and welfare of its members. It is financed by contributions, normally compulsory, which are graded according to the category of student. All college clubs and societies
are affiliated to the SU and it underwrites their activities. In
fact, its influence in student affairs is all-embracing and all-
pervasive.

It buys special items of equipment for societies, purchases
furnishings and magazines for the common rooms, and
provides trophies for happy occasions and wreaths for sad
ones. It backs the publication of the college magazine, arranges dances and concerts, and pays the expenses of college

teams. It collects money for Christmas parcels, organises Rags, provides the money for the college minibus, and subsidises the myriad activities of a sometimes unappreciative student body.

College holidays are similar in length to those of the schools and are taken at much the same time. The only difference is that we tend to start a week or two before the schools at the beginning of September and then finish correspondingly earlier in July. Half-term holidays in the autumn and winter terms are rather less common because of the administrative difficulties involved with so many different types of student.

The autumn term is a demanding one and the pressures build up quickly. Until the enrolment is over, we do not know exactly how many students we shall be getting, what courses will run, or what special options will be taken up. Mind you, we have a fair idea, based partly on experience and partly on the number of full-time students who have already been accepted for courses, yet many students wait till their A and O level results come out in August before finally deciding to take a college course. This has obvious repercussions on our internal organisation and September is a shocking month for heads of department. Although they may have done their timetables and allocated rooms, inevitably there are all kinds of alterations to be made, classes to be split or merged, extra staff to be taken on, and late arrivals to be interviewed. It sometimes seems that students and staff have hardly settled down after the maelstrom of September before December looms ahead.

December is the cruellest month with its welter of internal examinations, marking, and reports, all crowned by Christmas 'activities'. Christmas, despite the goodwill, remains a dangerous time. As we stagger towards the end of term, teachers are slightly off balance, kitchen staff are sweating blood, and even amiable caretakers get tetchy over decorations and shifting furniture about. Heads of department pull themselves up the stairs by the handrail while the principal, visibly ageing, looks like the Ghost of Christmas Past.

Yet at this point emerges the service-potential of our

students, a positive desire to help and contribute at this special time of year. Most SUs concentrate their activities on the old and the young. There are visits to entertain handicapped children, concerts for the blind, visits to the local hospital, and special teas or lunches for old-age-pensioners in the district. The girls enjoy propping the old ladies up on the landing and helping the old men up the stairs. Some of the old men enjoy it, too.

Many SUs collect for gift parcels which are delivered by hand to the housebound and infirm. 'By hand' is important. It is not the gift that matters (though in some cases it does) but the fact that someone knows and cares. These visits underline the affinity between youth and age. The conditions under which some of our old people live come as a shock to many students and it is not only the pensioners who are rather overwhelmed.

Having done their bit, the students turn to their own pleasures. The hall and refectory are dressed overall and the manageress and her staff brace themselves for the last lap of Christmas lunches. The students have decorated the hall, too, and they all squeeze in there for the carol service. This service is often arranged by a small group of staff and students with an *ad hoc* choir to lead the singing. The form of the service may be traditional or wildly unorthodox, the music may be Hely-Hutchinson or folk, but somehow the magic still survives. The lights glow on the Christmas tree at the side of the stage and we sing the old familiar carols. For a brief space we are a collegiate body and we all feel good, deep down good.

That evening sees the social climax of the year, the students' Christmas dance. A blast of hot angry sound, like a lion's breath, hits you as you push your way through the crowd round the door of the hall. Inside the lights are low and the air shudders as an imported group, curls damp with sweat, howls into the microphones. In the gloom, knots of students twitch and jerk to the compulsive pounding from the stage. You wave to the secretary of the SU (can that really be the secretary?) and beam goodwill at and over the vibrating figures. You struggle outside again. This is no place for you, man. Goodnight! Happy Christmas! Good-night! . . . God bless us, everyone . . .

January and February are fairly quiet months, if any period can be called quiet in the colleges. February sees most of the entries made for the various examining bodies: City and Guilds, Royal Society of Arts (for commercial subjects, always known as RSA), the regional examining unions, the various GCE boards, and, of course, for the national certificates and diplomas.

The end of this term is often chosen for the production of a play, since life becomes difficult after Easter what with revision and the endless examination period which may extend over eight weeks in a large college. Few colleges have actual courses in drama but some now present student productions, largely as a happy side effect of the growing number of full-time students on academic courses. Putting on a play is one of those occasions when students from all departments can be involved in designing, acting, building and painting the set, printing the programmes, or helping backstage.

This is not the only arts activity that flourishes during the session though it attracts most publicity. In many colleges the term is punctuated by recitals and exhibitions and your college may well act as a venue for a variety of cultural activities.

I realise I have said precious little so far about the library. This is, or should be, one of the mainsprings of any college, a learning and information centre at once satisfying yet stimulating. A library is not simply a room with rows and rows of dull old books, a few of which you have to read or consult during your course, but an exciting place in which to make discoveries and extend horizons. Both the status and the role of the library have grown considerably in FE in recent years as its importance has been recognised.

In effect the library is seen today, to use the fashionable phrase, as a resources centre for both staff and students. Indeed in some colleges the library is regarded simply as a major part of a resources centre which also includes what are called non-book materials. These consist of the 'hardware' i.e. audio-visual aids ranging from video-cassette recorders to film strip projectors, plus such associated 'software' as films, film strips, tapes and transparencies. The audio-visual aids and the software would ideally be situated adjacent to the library with an audio-visual aid technician to issue and maintain the equipment and to develop teaching aids for the staff. But because the concept arrived well after most colleges were built, audio-visual aids are either held departmentally or housed in some convenient central store.

Such a centre may have a Media Resources Officer or Learning Resources Officer in overall charge with the librarian as one of his team.

I have never yet met a librarian who was satisfied with his annual allowance and certainly compared with other countries the sums we allocate our libraries are curiously small. Still, FE does much better than the schools in this respect and students are impressed by the sheer physical size of the library and the diversity of the stock, particularly the range of periodicals.

Students on many of the full-time courses will have several 'free' periods for private study just like any sixth former. They usually spend these in the library since very few colleges possess any other places where students can sit down and work quietly on their own. Because of pressure of numbers on the library, students may find arrangements for private study made for them in the hall. It is not always easy to find somewhere they can work undisturbed.

Already at Easter the examinations are beginning to cast a long shadow. The day-release students, HNC, ONC, technician and craft, have now only a few more weeks of attendance before their examinations start during the week before Whitsun. When colleges re-open after the Whitsun holiday, the day of reckoning is upon the students with a vengeance.

Examination time is a massive administrative exercise for the college office. With hundreds, sometimes thousands, of students taking a multiplicity of subjects with a variety of examining bodies, it is an ordeal for the registrar. Providing accommodation, especially for the popular subjects, is a nightmare and halls, gymnasia and lecture theatres—

anywhere in fact that will house a sizeable number of students—are commandeered for weeks on end.

I often think the students' year starts with a bang and ends with a whimper. As the examinations grind on our students drop off in penny numbers. The GCE students usually depart as soon as their examinations begin to work privately at home while full-time students in other departments tend to stay on until their examinations are over.

As for the part-time students, once their examinations have finished they will attend for another week or so to go over the papers but this is about all. In theory the last couple of attendances left in the session could be spent on exploring certain parts of the syllabus in greater depth, or introducing next year's work, or on minor projects. In practice employers are reluctant to send their employees to college after the examinations and the employees are equally reluctant to attend classes which in their view no longer have any point. They are great ones for relevance! Staff, too, at the end of a hard session show little inclination for such amiable suggestions and, like Moses, ask only that their people be allowed to go.

Thus the session subsides rather than closes. Day by day the part-time courses fall off until finally only some of the full-time students remain. These, in turn, depart, not as they had probably imagined in a blaze of jollity and good-fellowship, but quietly and sometimes sadly.

For many it is the end of full-time education and they are bound inexorably for the great outside. There will be one last long summer holiday and then nothing will ever be quite the same again. Other students are going on to universities, polytechnics, and colleges of education. For them there will be a sense of excitement and expectation tinged only by a faint frisson of unease at leaving the familiar small pool for the uncharted sea.

So all depart—well, not quite all. There are still some block-release students and lads on industrial training courses haunting the building and they press steadily on until the end of July. But they, too, leave in due course and for a brief while, perhaps all of four weeks, the college is strangely silent.

Then suddenly it's September and the patter of feet in the corridors mounts to a deafening roar. Seed-time again!

CHAPTER NINE

The spirit

*Except the Lord build the house, their labour is but
lost that build it.*

Psalm CXXVII

Colleges of FE don't have chapels. King's College has its
chapel and public schools all over England have their
chapels, soaring heavenwards in neo-gothic splendour and
bathing the wealthy siblings in a dim religious glow. But you
will search in vain for the chapel at Slyme Green College of
Further Education. Not that I imagine you would expect to
find one. In the past technical education, serving the needs
of industry and commerce on a part-time basis, was never
swayed by such considerations.

It is not surprising then that scant attention was paid to
this aspect of education as the full-time population of the
colleges rapidly expanded in the 'fifties and 'sixties. It never
crossed the mind of most principals, and many of the older
ones, more at home with a hacksaw than a hymn book, saw
little point in disturbing further the uneven tenor of their way
by dabbling in organised or disorganised religion.

Thus today you will find little trace of formal religious
observance in our colleges. Most staff in FE believe it is
wrong to attempt to expose young adults at the eleventh hour
to beliefs and ideas they have been steadily rejecting or
ignoring at school and work for years. These colleagues
might admit, under pressure and with some reluctance, that
the life of a college should reflect the Christian ethic, but it
would be with the uneasy feeling of leaving the door open for
cant and humbug to creep in. They feel that assemblies for
quasi-religious purposes (which have never been part of FE
anyway) belong essentially to the world of school and should
play no part in the life of an institution which purports to be
adult and different and deals with an age range used to a

considerable degree of freedom and choice. This view seems to be shared by nearly all the students.

On the other hand, there is a small number of people who think that further education is enriched and strengthened by being seen to be taking place against a Christian background, the more effective for being unobtrusive. They believe that colleges have a responsibility for the moral and spiritual needs of their students and should make some attempt to meet them. Their efforts meet with little success because of the disinterest of most staff and the reactions of the students, which vary from apathy to hostility.

A few of our colleges have chaplains. These are not full-time members of the teaching staff (though it is a help if you have a lecturer in holy orders) but local clergy acting in an honorary capacity. The main difficulty lies in integrating them with the life of the college. There are several ways of trying to do this. One is for the chaplains to be available for consultation by students at a certain time each week—a kind of clerical surgery. Clergy are busy people and have sudden compelling demands made upon their time, so it is not always easy for them to be in the same place at the same time every week. Even if they are, experience suggests that they are rarely consulted. Most of our students have had no effective contact with the church for years and are unaccustomed to the idea of turning to the clergy for help. Another way is to employ the special skills and training of the chaplains as part-time teachers. They can be used in general studies periods to deal with comparative religion, or, more often, to lead discussions about personal relationships. They can also take part in occasional confrontations, still under the broad wing of general studies, with groups of students.

The chaplains are always seeking other ways in which to help. They are very conscious that with the limited time at their disposal they are only reaching a minority and their influence is slight. Their mere physical presence in the college on occasions other than carol services is the outward and visible sign, vestigial admittedly, of a striving for something a little more effective.

Even if they do not run to honorary chaplains, many colleges have branches, flourishing and otherwise, of the Student Christian Movement. The SCM, run by a small band of enthusiastic staff and students, invites local speakers, holds discussion groups, and provides a focus for Christian interest in the college.

Although there are few signs in the average college of any interest in religion, there is a considerable amount of informal Christian activity. Our young people have a vast fund of altruism. They are easily moved by want and distress and are eager to translate their idealism into rapid and practical action. This intense concern for others less fortunate than themselves has almost become the prerogative of this age group. Part of our job as teachers is to harness such concern and turn it into useful fields of endeavour. In this the Students' Union can be a great help. I have dealt earlier with its role in the college but its influence is pervasive and it keeps cropping up and demanding attention in other contexts.

Go into any college and on the notice board you will almost certainly find a poster about some charitable effort. This week it may be Christian Aid or Save the Children Fund; next week, Oxfam or a sponsored walk in aid of some local charity. Last year, an earthquake fund; this year, famine relief. Always the emphasis is on giving, on involvement, with the needs of the very old or the very young uppermost.

As we have seen, student effort is at its most obvious at Christmas when many Students' Unions organise the delivery of parcels to pensioners and those in need. If the drama club puts on a Christmas play, then there is a matinée for the old-age-pensioners and old people are often invited to a special meal at the college. Other students visit the housebound and the lonely in hospital while student groups entertain at old people's and children's homes. It is not difficult to spread the idea of voluntary service to the community within a college. The difficulty is to spread the response more evenly over the year.

These are the unpublicised activities, unheralded, unsung acts of kindness and compassion which rarely make the headlines. In many huge colleges on the other hand the Students' Unions run highly publicised Rag Weeks and collect vast sums of money for local charities. These Rags make a considerable impact. Television stars are willingly abducted, shopkeepers intimidated, traffic disrupted, exotic competitions and unusual vehicles become the order of the day, and encouraging slogans appear in the most inaccessible places. The students get up to all kinds of stunts artfully designed to wheedle money from the pockets of the public. Occasionally, and it is only very occasionally, some prank misfires through the madness of the moment and brings down the wrath of the press and the local ratepayers upon the principal. No matter, he is born unto trouble as the sparks fly upward.

These colourful, charitable efforts of the Students' Unions do a service in promoting a favourable student image and go a long way towards making the college part of the life of the area it serves. At a time when a tiny fraction of students in higher education are attracting unfavourable publicity, it is refreshing to regard the other side of the coin.

Let us now turn to pastoral care, that delightful concept, which is by no means the monopoly of the secondary schools. A charge frequently levelled against colleges of FE is that they pay little attention to this aspect. Certainly, pastoral care, or concern for the moral and social welfare of young people, is not a phrase you hear being bandied about in college staffrooms. Looking round our colleges, a visitor might exclaim 'What flocks!'—though not, I trust, 'What shepherds!'—and wonder whether this concept could conceivably impinge at any point upon our vivid cross-section of young people.

A few of my colleagues would indignantly deny that pastoral care is any part of our job and insist it belongs to the world of school. There are some in FE to whom the idea of pastoral care is unfamiliar, irrelevant, or unattractive. Because of our origins it was never possible for it to become one of our traditions. Yet, although this feeling still exists, it is outweighed by the rapidly growing emphasis being placed on student welfare. This may be a side effect of the increase in full-time students. There is nothing like a large full-time student body to bring home to staff the realisation of what it means to be a teacher in the fullest sense. Certainly most of us in FE have taken a welcome leaf out of the schools' book and we now regard the welfare of our students as an important part of our work. Staff have moved outside the workshop in their thinking—another of the significant developments of recent years.

In the colleges our thinking revolves round the utilitarian 'welfare' rather than the classical 'pastoral care'. If our concern manifests itself in ways different from those in the schools, this is only natural and proper and what you, gentle reader, would by now expect. Concern there certainly is and I would hate to leave you with the idea that colleges shrug off their responsibilities simply by appointing a nurse for first-aid and a lodgings officer charged specially with 'welfare'.

I used this word 'concern' in the last paragraph. In one of its little booklets on FE, the DES, describing the relationship between staff and students, coined a phrase I should have been proud to father—'informed concern'. If every teacher in a college had this attribute, then principals would lay their greying heads upon the pillow at night and sleep like babes. The encouraging thing is that so many teachers now have it.

How is our concern for student welfare translated into action? The normal arrangement in colleges is for every full-time course to have a course tutor. This is often the teacher who spends most time with the class and therefore has most opportunity to get to know the students individually. It is to the course tutor in the first instance that students turn if they are having difficulty with their work or have a personal problem. Many students may well approach their head of department over difficulties with their course of study but few, I suspect, would ask his advice over a personal matter. In this case a student will either talk to his course tutor or seek the counsel of some sympathetic member of staff.

The course tutor system is also extended to the day-release students and it is usual for a member of staff to be given this responsibility either for a single course or for a group of part-time day courses. Day-release students do not appear to have the problems encountered by a few of our full-time students or if they do, they seek to solve them through, or obtain advice about them from, agencies other than the college. Even so, there are occasions when the braggadocio crumbles and they come to us for help.

From this you can see that the course tutor, rather like the form-master or mistress, is a father or mother figure. Many course tutors are finding they are not sufficiently equipped or experienced to deal with the range of personal problems erupting among the older students. This has led to much interest recently in the idea of counselling and some colleges have appointed full-time teacher/counsellors. Others, taking advantage of the short and long courses in counselling run by the DES and by LEAs are developing various arrangements to meet student needs.

I hope we shall keep a sense of proportion about counselling and not be misled by the mass-media into believing that all young adults in the 16 to 21 age range are introverted, drug-ridden, frustrated neurotics, needing the services of some guru in a cupboard. If you look around our colleges, most of the students are happy, sensible, purposive individuals who need letting alone more than anything else. True, they are suffering, as we all did, the splendours and miseries of adolescence, but I would be reluctant to counsel them out of this particular experience.

For most young adults this is the period of pre-occupation with sex and many colleges attempt to deal positively with some of the problems young people face. It is not easy and there is an uneven foundation to build upon. Sex education is handled differently, diffidently, or not at all in the secondary schools and one has some sympathy with the teachers there for being saddled with a responsibility which is rightly the parents'. Aware, like our colleagues in the schools, of the ignorance about sexual matters among teenagers, we try to help by dealing with sex education in terms of personal relationships. Many students find unemotional talks on the physical aspects of sex helpful and from these spring discussions about the problems of courtship and marriage. But there is always the problem of time and numbers and it is only possible to reach a small percentage of our students.

Naturally this work must be undertaken by a nucleus of willing and sympathetic teachers supported by suitably qualified part-time help. Some colleges have established links with the local Marriage Guidance Council and their counsellors help with the discussion work. I only wish there were more of these invaluable people about to help us during the day.

In this chapter I have mentioned some examples of the practical steps we take, hesitant and unsure though they often are at first, to help our students with their difficulties. We cannot stand *in loco parentis* (this phrase has never been much in vogue in colleges anyway) but most staff are coming to see themselves in the role of friendly advisers. Thus we are steadily establishing a framework for student care. Our aim is to make as many lifelines available as possible and to give full-time and part-time students every encouragement to reach out for them in time of trouble.

Our attempts to help are always changing direction, always under discussion, always seeking greater effectiveness. We know our limitations only too well and how far we still have to go—but colleges do care.

CHAPTER TEN

The flesh

'During the fourteen years I have been here', said the Doctor, *'there have been six sports days, all of them, in one way or another, utterly disastrous.'*

Decline and Fall Evelyn Waugh

Traditionally, physical education has no role in technical education. During the first forty years of this century most students in technical education received their education in the evenings in institutions which rarely boasted a gymnasium. They may have had a hall which was used for various purposes but never for organised physical education. What, never? Well hardly ever. There was simply no time. It never occurred to anyone to make time.

It was only with the development of part-time day and full-time courses after the war that any serious attention began to be paid by a few enthusiasts to PE. Many principals and their staffs ignored it and even today there are still thousands of technical teachers of all persuasions who declare they fail to see what purpose it serves and what use it is to their students.

The cause of physical education has not been helped either by the attitude of the employers. Industry's view has been, as always, refreshingly direct. If they were giving a lad a day off (with pay) to further his studies and thereby make himself more useful to them, then physical education was superfluous. It was mathematics and science and workshop technology they wanted to see, not their lads playing games in working hours. By and large this prejudice has been overcome and physical education is now an accepted part of the curriculum. In fact, as we shall see, the employers seem to have transferred their hostility from physical education to general studies, fortunately with the same lack of success.

Such was the unpromising background against which physical education fought for respectability and acceptance.

It was helped by a slowly growing realisation that if technical education was to be effective in preparing a student to play his part in modern society, then it would have to lay much more emphasis than hitherto on the development of all aspects of the individual. This is old hat educational theory but it was tingling fresh so far as further education was concerned. The importance of PE (and its traditional justification) is that every student, just as he is encouraged to develop his mental faculties to the full, should be able to develop physical skills for the pleasure and sense of well-being derived from them.

By the middle 'fifties, the expansion of further education was well under way and the new buildings had either spacious and well-equipped gymnasia or dual purpose halls. Admittedly the gymnasia in many cases were regrettably little used (except for examinations) since a number of principals brought up in the old hard school were simply uninterested in developing this side of their work. Even today, when technical education has come of age, physical education remains something of a puking infant, undeveloped and struggling hard to make its needs known.

For despite the rash of new buildings, there is still a long way to go. In 1963, a survey by the Association of Technical Institutions* revealed that only half our colleges at that time possessed a gymnasium. And although three-quarters of them had access to playing fields, again only half had their own—and these were not always on the same site. Obviously the position has improved substantially since then but it would be interesting to know by how much.

It all depends on facilities. When these are available most full-time students, male and female, normally have provision made for PE on their timetable. But how many part-time students have PE as part of their course? Not a great number I suspect. Most colleges have only one gymnasium and if this is available, say for ten hours each day from 9 a.m. to 7 p.m., then fifty hours is not a vast amount of time to play with and the full-time courses naturally take precedence.

* Reported in *Sports Facilities in Technical Colleges* by D. B. Bartlett, then Chief Education Officer, Southend.

You may wonder why so many post-war colleges have rather old-fashioned gymnasia. Perhaps the answer is that no one at the planning stage ever sat down and considered whether what was appropriate for a school was necessarily appropriate for the needs of a college with a high proportion of its students in the 18–21 age range—and some of them great, hefty lads at that. As a result we were saddled with the school-type gymnasium complete with wallbars, beams and climbing ladders.

However, in recent years we have seen the emergence and development of the sports hall. This is the largest area you can afford, devoid of impedimenta, roofed over and well-lit. In some cases one complete side wall can be removed so that in reasonable weather the area immediately outside, which is often a hard surface playing area, becomes an extension of indoors. Ideally, a sports hall should be 120 ft by 60 ft but most colleges have to be satisfied with a good deal less. It provides the area needed to play any of the five major indoor games (tennis, basketball, netball, badminton and volley-ball) which the pre-war (and post-war) standard gymnasium (66 ft by 30 ft, giving roughly 2,000 sq ft) was quite unable to do.

The sports hall also provides all-the-year-round, day and evening, facilities for practice and recreation—and if there are refreshment rooms and lounges attached so much the better. It is, I feel, only this type of highly flexible building which is capable of meeting the increasing demand by students and the public for more and better physical recreational facilities.

I have had a little experience of trying to reconcile an intractable gym with a burning desire to do great things. In 1961, I became principal of Newton-le-Willows College of Further Education, a small local college, typical of many in the North of England which had developed from junior technical schools established just before the First World War.

I went there without any prejudice against physical education since it had never occurred to me for one moment that any curriculum could ignore PE and be successful. PT and games were mother's milk to me.

I looked round and took stock. I was not exactly embarrassed with riches. The college had a single-sex gymnasium built in 1937. It was a child of its time, about 60 ft by 30 ft, with the usual wallbars, window ladders and beams but, alas, no store. There was a grubby changing room, a depressing urinal, and some evil-looking showers. It would have made an excellent set for shots of prisoners showering on arrival at the Scrubs.

At the back of the college within the boundary railings there was enough grass for a football pitch for dwarfs. But, since there was solid clay a foot under the surface, for most of the year it was a morass and quite unusable. It would have made excellent paddy fields. I found that if we wanted to play football properly then we had to reserve a pitch on a local playing field a mile away. I suppose we were lucky it was only a mile away.

None of the apprentices had any PE. A number of the girls enjoyed ill-defined 'games', but that was about all. However, the male PE teacher was progressive and enthusiastic and so were his part-time female colleagues. So first of all we set about the gym. We removed the window ladders at one end, leaving the blank wall beloved of advisers. We took out all the beams, but shied at removing the wallbars which, although not used much, at least protected the windows. New, powerful lamps replaced the Toc H ones and with the ceiling painted blue, the walls pale grey and the floor sanded and polished, we were ready to establish PE on a proper footing for our young men and girls.

Girls, of course, present a special difficulty. Some of these otherwise soft and tractable creatures who come to us have a marked distaste for team games, exercise work, athletics and, dare it be said, for the kind of modern dance now being developed at the specialist training colleges for PE teachers.

There is, of course, the problem of a suitably feminine outfit, one that will be suitable for various kinds of activity. The traditional shorts are not popular with plump parties and not easy to find in the shops if you are WX, that most intriguing of formulae. Many girls dislike short skirts for outside wear since the wind is apt to lift them just as the more highly strung lads are passing. Since we make no attempt to impose uniformity, girls continue to wear either skirts or shorts, according to taste, with a variety of tops. One of the popular outfits at present is the slimline nylon tracksuit which is attractive and allows a good range of movement.

And then there is the question of approach. Despite what I said just now about the attitude of some of them towards PE, most girls, even the most sinuous and *soignée*, enjoy playing games of some sort, and those who actively enjoy PE and have some natural talent are keen to increase their personal performance and try new activities from the range available to them in the gymnasium.

The secret lies in a positive, personal approach. A skilled and sympathetic teacher will first discuss with a class of new female students the range of opportunities available and the type of activity that interests them. There are no compulsory games like hockey or netball. The teacher will attempt to achieve a blend of games and group work in which the whole class can join, together with activities designed to foster individual skills.

The approach with young men is similar though they are generally more enthusiastic about team games, particularly five-a-side football which they will play until they drop. This feverish interest in soccer provides the teacher with a key to open the door to higher things.

The argument runs thus. To be effective at any team game (and this applies also to exacting individual pursuits like cycling, weightlifting, athletics and squash) demands a high level of physical fitness. This can only be achieved by a regular programme of coordinated exercises and activities. Young men will therefore accept the rigours of circuit training as a means to an end. For some they become an agreeable means to no particular end except that of keeping in good physical trim. Many apprentices, desperate about football, are willing to come back on one evening a week for fitness training which is a mixture of circuit train-ing and exercises. And this is now being done to music.

But I would not like you to feel that it is football, football all the way. For many young men the facilities of a modern gymnasium spark off all kinds of new interests. Few, for example, have ever been able to fence before or try their hand at weightlifting or trampolining. Basketball and volleyball are also very popular. Most athletic youngsters take to badminton like ducks to water—even though they may have thought it a pretty effeminate game. A growing number of students who have no recognisable talents for the usual team games and possess little natural ball skill find a satisfaction in individual pursuits (golf, cross-country running, archery) they never previously associated with the crisp, brisk outline of PE.

Thus the teacher achieves one of his basic aims: giving the students an interest which they can develop as a pleasurable leisure activity in the future.

Of course, much depends on where the college is situated. My college is close to the River Dee and not far from the Welsh hills. This means that during the week and at weekends we can offer activities such as swimming, sub-aqua and canoeing. Every college will have a different range of options.

This emphasis in colleges on the development of the individual and his introduction to as wide a range of activities as possible makes strenuous demands upon the teacher. No longer does he merely have to know about cricket, soccer and athletics. He must be knowledgeable about, and preferably able to coach, most physical activities. He or she has to organise the PE period in such a way as to satisfy the ambitions (or whims) of the class as individuals and yet ensure they indulge in a healthy amount of group activities. He has to cater for the athletic and the apathetic, for the aggressive and the non-competitive. Not always very easy.

Teachers also seek to stimulate interest in physical education at lunch-times and in the evenings. In many colleges the gymnasium is open during the lunch hour and students can drift in and out to sample various activities. Because of the demand some colleges are reserving their gymnasia for two or three nights a week for their own students. Young people find this informal programming attractive.

I am not a great one for giving long lists but I have cunningly mentioned quite a number of games and activities so far in this chapter. Most of these a student may properly expect to be available during his course. I must admit I found it difficult to come to terms with table tennis as a proper activity but I have been educated into it.

So far I have not mentioned cricket. It grieves me beyond measure that this noble, subtle game is sick unto death in the colleges. In a fairly large college like mine we have difficulty in raising a team even with a stiffening (if that is the right term) of members of staff. For reasons that are as obvious as they are saddening interest in the game appears to be as much on the wane in colleges as it is in the schools.

What is the relation between physical education in colleges and community needs? Just as I see the college as the cultural and leisure focus of the area it serves, so the role of the PE department cannot be restricted to the college. We all know there is a booming interest in physical recreational activities. Sailing, climbing, golf, skiing have never been so popular and there is an increasing demand for coaching and practice facilities in all sports. In most areas only the local college or the better-equipped schools can provide these. In addition many local sports clubs are having difficulty in finding suitable premises for their own pursuits and look to the college for help.

Therefore I see the development of leisure education continuing in FE in the next few years with staff seeking to make the college the recreational centre for the locality. Since money is so tight, it seems sensible to concentrate on expanding the natural centres (the local and area colleges) where good facilities already exist, rather than invest in expensive independent leisure centres.

So it would be prudent in future when colleges have the rare privilege of laying out their playing fields to think in terms of area provision. The important thing is not to get lumbered with the kind of standard lay-out that the schools have. Our needs are very different and since no one knows much about what kind of facilities colleges should have, we must strive to see that what we consider proper provision is made at the outset. Besides space for the usual team games, we should insist on a running track (so sorely needed) with an all-weather playing area inside it. This whole area needs to be floodlit so that it can be used at night during the eight long, dark months, for this is when facilities are really needed by young people—and not only the young. I should like to see these outdoor facilities developed in conjunction with the sports hall, which should have squash courts and (if funds allow) a swimming pool attached to it. What I want is not a fun palace, but a sports palace—a centre for all kinds of interesting and exciting activities for people in the college catchment area.

Talking of running tracks, few colleges today are bold or mad enough to hold sports days. We used to at Newton-le-Willows. Since we had no playing fields of our own, we had to borrow a delightful little ground belonging to the Viaduct Sports Institute. In this oasis, tucked away in a desert of Victorian terrace houses, there was a cricket field upon which we painted our track, and two small pavilions (his and hers) with opportunities for teas, light refreshments, and minerals. The ground was beautifully kept and the green turf, white benches and pink pavilions were as rivers of water in a dry land. Here on summer afternoons retired railwaymen used to sit in the sun, lean their chins on their sticks, and dream of steam.

Beyond the field were bowling greens and tennis courts policed at intervals by statues of neat-breasted nymphs and under-developed youths. By the drinking fountain there was a statue of an earnest-looking character with long hair, a hard hat and a concussed expression. I never found out who he was, but he could have been on the council.

Although committed to athletics, especially for others, it is not my ideal spectator sport. The spirit soon wearies of hairy-legged lads tearing round and round the field—chaps doing laps—and I find a little goes a long way. I was never a Simon Pure Three As man. I must admit I like to see the tedium of endless sprints and what have you broken up by such jolly events as sack races, obstacle races, three-legged races and so forth. What the purists label gymkhana events.

I managed to convert my PE teachers to this view (principals can be unscrupulous at times) and the most popular event was the invitation mixed three-legged race. In my last year this was won by a blonde pneumatic catering student and one of the young male staff. I am still not sure how he managed to enter but we all thought he fully deserved the prize.

I saw five sports days there and they were five of the coldest, windiest and most miserable May afternoons I have ever struck. By tradition, and for convenience, sports day was held on a Friday afternoon a little before Whitsun, when the weather was thought to be fairly stable.

Not so. On the Thursday night before what came to be known as Black Friday, there was always a downpour which washed out our carefully drawn white lines. We spent the forenoon feverishly re-painting the lines, re-erecting the public address system and repairing the ravages of the night. All the time a pall of grey cloud remained stationary over the town.

We went armed. My shooting stick, originally produced to give a Country Life flavour to the afternoon, soon gave way to an umbrella. Overcoat, scarf and gloves were *de rigueur* and the staff appeared looking ready to tackle the north face of the Eiger. One year it was so cold in May we had to have hot soup sent down from the college.

I also inherited two starters-cum-helpers. One was an aged railway pensioner, a dear old chap, full of athletic feats seen on the ground in days gone by. His companion was a much younger man called Sid, who wore a cap so loud it did audible damage to our professional image.

Sid used to bring the pistol. This looked rather like the gun that won the West and it had a knack of producing a loud click at the moment of truth and then going off in Sid's pocket half a minute later. Not once did it last the whole meeting and by 2.45 p.m. we were always back to using Sid's hankie.

The gaiety of the afternoon reached its climax with a rousing tug-of-war between twelve choice pre-nursing students and eight likely lads from the engineering department.

O Loughborough, my Loughborough! We never actually got as far as an egg-and-spoon race, but I was being
sounded about a slow-bicycle race the summer I left.

After the tug-of-war, the students clustered round the
table by the loudspeaker and I presented the prizes. We used
to break all the rules and jeopardise everybody's amateur
status by giving small cash prizes, which were immediately
translated into cream cakes, chocolate and cigarettes round
the corner.

Then we posed for photographs for the local paper. We
usually made the front page because nothing much ever
happened there in May. Smile, please! A big smile, now!
This was the moment the sullen clouds chose to empty
themselves upon us. There was a mad dash for cover. We
all got soaked and sports day was over for another year.

I like to think that in the larger colleges it is a little less
homely, much more purposeful and that standard times are
infinitely higher. I only hope it is as enjoyable. There is a
danger sometimes of physical education becoming just a
little too clinical and sterile for comfort.

The physical education work in a college has an importance, especially to the principal, that it is not always
apparent. Under sympathetic and energetic leadership, the
physical education electives spark off all kinds of clubs and
extra-curricular activities. At week-ends there are rock
climbing and camping expeditions, canoeing, angling, and
sailing trips. During the holidays there are skiing parties and
visits abroad. All this activity helps to promote that sense
of belonging which, as we saw in an earlier chapter, is so
difficult to create in a college with a transient population.
This is the special contribution of PE.

We have been talking so far in this chapter about the
development of the human machine. But machines need fuel
and it is time to look at that most interesting part of the
college, the refectory. Most new students are baffled by this
rather superior word. Those coming straight from school
have been accustomed to a dining-room or hall; those
coming in on day-release have recently experienced the
delights of the works canteen. Refectory has a monkish,

academic flavour, subtly predisposing the student to a certain plainness and monotony in the fare. But you could not be more wrong. There is a shattering change from the *table d'hôte* of the school dinner to the *à la carte* of the refectory. You hear very few grumbles about the food from the students in colleges. Like most young people, they can recognise a good thing when they see it.

Most colleges now have large airy refectories with cafeteria service. Yet large as they are, they are not large enough. The accommodation has simply not kept pace with the rapid increase in students and most refectories I know are, like my own, grossly overcrowded. We do not, of course, have 'sittings'; we try to overcome the problem by staggering the times at which the various departments finish their morning's work.

There are all kinds of minor shifts and devices a principal can employ to get the maximum number of students passing through the refectory in the shortest possible time. But even after all this, there is still an unreasonable and inescapable amount of queueing in most colleges because of the sheer weight of numbers. There is little opportunity for civilised eating with a leisurely smoke and chat over a cup of coffee afterwards. It's a case of sup up, shut up and get up, for there is a long queue behind casting envious eyes on your place. It takes a student an average of twelve and a half minutes to dispose of a main course and sweet from the 'off', so gracious living is rather at a discount. Some colleges are fortunate in having student lounges or separate coffee shops but the run-of-the-mill colleges can only look covetously at facilities like these. Sometimes all they can offer are overcrowded common rooms with vending machines.

Fortunately the food is satisfactory, otherwise these accommodation difficulties would cause no little discontent. It is the same in any organisation. If the food is right then your tiny problems remain tiny problems. But if it isn't, then you are stuck with a festering sore which tends to inflame the slightest disaffection in the college. (By one who knows.) At my first college I had a stream of complaints, most of them justified, about the food. This led to a series of rather stormy interviews with my cook-supervisor, *une femme formidable*—one of the many privileges a principal enjoys. It takes a great deal of moral fibre for an ageing lightweight to tangle with a massive cook straight out of *Alice in Wonderland*. After she vanished the food improved and several other little local difficulties disappeared as well.

At lunch-time students are able to choose from a wide range of main dishes, snacks and sweets. Full-time students under 19 pay the going rate for school dinners for a two course meal, but older students and day-release students normally choose whatever takes their fancy and pay for it accordingly. And there are always other items available such as soup, pies, fruit, cakes, ice-cream, cheese and biscuits, plus hot and cold drinks. The range and attractiveness of the dishes are related directly to the ability and imagination of the manageress. A capable manageress is a pearl of great price. If you have one, hug her to your bosom. Never mind the smell of frying.

The reputation of a college does not rest solely upon academic excellence, however much the purists think. The promise of good food is a bait not to be despised. This is particularly true of all those local and national bodies who like to use our premises, bringing with their custom potential customers, and fathers and mothers of potential customers.

We have so far been talking only about lunch, but our refectory service does not stop there. Colleges are going full blast for over twelve hours a day and the refectory services have to be geared to these conditions. Apart from lunch, there are the mid-morning and afternoon breaks, and then there are teas and evening meals to be served. Teas can vary from the dainty to the spectacular. Evening meals are very popular with many students who come to evening classes straight from work without a chance to get home for a meal —and our food is cheaper and often more attractive than what they can buy outside. Similarly, many students finishing a busy day at the college prefer to have a meal in the refectory before facing a longish journey home. Some colleges serving rural areas even open early to serve breakfast and if a college has a large programme of leisure courses in the evenings there will sometimes be a break with students clamouring for coffee. Thus the service will vary according to the nature of the student body and the type of area the college serves. In our larger colleges the refectory is a bustling lively place providing a continuous service; in the small and medium-sized colleges it is only open at certain times during the day.

Because a refectory has to meet such varied needs, most local authorities accept that it is unreasonable for it to be either wholly self-supporting or profit-making. There is usually some form of subsidy, the most common being the waiving of certain overheads. Treasurers are tolerably happy (no treasurer is ever wholly happy about anything connected with FE) if the refectory takes enough money to cover staff wages and the cost of the food.

The school dinner attempts to provide a balanced diet spread over a week and the reasons for this are laudable and obvious. Colleges have never had to bother about this because for years most students attended for only one day per week. Now there is a great full-time student population we simply give the customers what they want. Some take a normal two course meal while others delight in combinations and permutations of the various items available. But always with chips! Mounds of glistening, golden chips! Particularly in the north-west which is real chip-country. They have egg and chips, fish and chips, sausage and chips, chop and chips, and, best-loved of all, pie and chips. And for the chip buffs, it's just chips, solus, in single or in double portions.

Come to that, I am rather fond of chips myself.

CHAPTER ELEVEN

General education : general studies : adult education

Studies serve for delight, for ornament, and for ability.

Of Studies Bacon

If you are a parent with a son doing his A levels at a college of FE, he will tell you he is in the general education department and you will not be very much the wiser. If you are a housewife going to a cookery class every Wednesday night, then your class will be run, although you will probably not be aware of it, by the general education department. If you are an employer with one or two apprentices attending college you will probably go purple in the face at the mention of 'general studies', which forms part of their day-release course and is taught by staff from the general education department. Like the dancer of whom it was said:

'She wore a tiny piece of tulle

That was like a red rag to a bull'

so, too, with general studies and the employer. All these apparently unrelated activities take place under the banner of the general education department. This department has four main functions. First, it runs the full-time GCE courses in the arts and sciences at A and O level and also the numerous part-time GCE courses offered during the day and evening.

Secondly, it is responsible for servicing all the other departments for English and general studies. That is, it provides the specialist staff and takes responsibility for the subject. So if a day-release engineering course has a general studies period in its timetable, or a secretarial course has several English periods in its curriculum, then these are taken by lecturers from the general education department.

You all know what an English period is but I wonder if you have any idea what I mean by general studies. Let us dwell a little on it because it is important. Attempts to define it usually lead to confusion and argument. The term seems to mean all things to all men. Let me try to explain by creeping up on it, as it were, in a roundabout fashion.

In the past when further education meant mainly part-time day and evening classes, the curriculum consisted, as you would expect, of technical subjects—mathematics, science, engineering drawing and workshop technology. There was no physical education, no English, not even any 'social studies'. And no thought of including any. Employers, employees, and nearly all teaching staff thought of these subjects, if they thought of them at all, as irrelevant.

However, during the expansion of the 1950s, serious doubts arose among educationists, including a few in the colleges, over whether what we were providing in the way of education for our technical students was in fact good enough. The vocational content seemed satisfactory, but was this by itself an adequate preparation for students taking their place in a rapidly changing and increasingly intricate society? We began to doubt if it was.

Did we not have a major responsibility to students in employment to ensure that they were prepared, so far as we could effect it in a very short time, for some of the difficulties about to beset them at work and in their private lives? Could we ignore the role of trade unions, the impact and influence of the mass-media, problems of constructive leisure, questions of morals and personal relationships? Should our students not have some idea of the way in which society organises itself, how the country is governed at both national and local level, together with some appreciation of the main social and political issues of our time?

You may well say that most of these topics are covered at school. Most are, but we are dealing with young adults from a broad band of ability and the knowledge of many of our craft and technician students of history, geography, and government is sketchy in the extreme.

Moreover, the standard of these students' written English is also often lamentable, reflecting a limited vocabulary and an inability to express themselves effectively in speech. Yet there is clearly a need in industry and commerce for better communication through the written and the spoken word. At work our students have to give instructions, write reports, pass on information and exchange ideas. The purpose of communication is to convey meaning and our students should be able to do this clearly, simply and briefly. Had we no responsibility here?

The answer was clear. Technology by itself was no longer enough and thus the infant general studies came unloved into a cold, unwelcoming world to redress the balance. From 1956 there was an element of general studies included in all day-release classes and it began to play a more important part in the curriculum of the full-time courses.

General studies had a difficult start. It suffered understandably from the lack of clearly stated aims and objectives and this made it easy meat for the Philistines.

The employers resisted stoutly. 'Why should I', said the hard-faced men from the smoky valleys, 'pay for my lads to come to the tech to learn about communism or play bloody football?' We paraded the familiar arguments. We as educationists and they as employers had a responsibility to these young employees to make some effort even at this late stage to make them more complete as individuals, more aware as citizens, and more effective as workers. We won, but the employers took a long time to adjust and even now there are occasional outbursts from the backwoodsmen.

It was not only the employers who were awkward. Many of our technical teachers, especially the die-hards in building and engineering, were unconvinced of the need for general studies and contemptuous of their role. And some still are, and say so.

At that time general studies (then called 'liberal studies') was seen essentially as an additive to the part-time vocational courses, a magic ingredient that would broaden and 'liberalise' the curriculum. It was all very hazy and ill-defined and attempts to define the term led to fascinating and endless

A rich and satisfying programme of leisure courses for adults—yet another function of FE colleges.

Variety is the keynote of FE in its extensive range of evening classes.

Adult dressmaking students getting down to basics.

Nursery—nursing students develop their musical talents.

A friendly chat with parents about their child's future helps to establish good relations.

debates on the aims of education. English, both language and literature, emerged as the heart, the core subject, of general studies, plus the study of man in relation to the society in which he lives and works. And to these elements of history, economics, sociology, theology, and geography was added physical education, because it was a part of our declared philosophy of attempting to develop the whole individual.

Slowly the ends and the means began to be clarified by conferences and articles, meetings and discussions, and through the influence of the Association for Liberal Education. Inevitably, regional examining bodies introduced examinations—always a sign of recognition—though whether examinations in general studies are desirable, except as a means of emphasising their respectability to other departments and impressing students with their sense of purpose, I beg leave to doubt.

This concept of general studies was accepted for a while but in the event it proved somewhat unsatisfactory and there has been a marked shift in recent years. Instead of general studies being regarded as a woolly liberal topping-up element, it is being broken down into more clearly identified components such as industrial studies and communications (writing, speaking and drawing). More important, there is now an emphasis on achieving the desired effect by a 'liberal' approach informing both the curriculum and the way it is taught. Colleges are seeking to broaden both part-time and full-time courses by introducing a more liberal content in to the curriculum and by more liberal teaching of both main and related subjects. I think the former is much easier to achieve than the latter, and you may well ask what precisely 'liberal' means in both contexts. It will be interesting to see how successful these new approaches prove.

The length of time spent upon general studies varies quite considerably but it is usually about an hour per week for part-time students. Obviously there is more time available in full-time courses and more ambitious work can be attempted. Much will depend upon the attitute of the head of department and how important the principal feels general studies to be. With increasing specialisation in technical subjects, and with more and more matter being crammed into the syllabuses, time is precious and general studies are always first to be thrown out of the balloon. Principals have to stand firm against the importunings of their heads of department.

Not all our students are enthralled by the prospect of general studies either. The younger day-release students, the 16 and 17 year olds, are inclined to look upon this period, if not exactly as a welcome break, then as the quiet hour for chat and relaxation. This is the time to dump their helmets and gauntlets on the desk, stretch out their legs, and invite the lecturer to entertain them on topics of the day. It is, they feel, better than working even if it is a bit boring and irrelevant. These are difficult classes to teach by any standard and it needs skilled and experienced staff to do so effectively. Then at about the age of 18 there is a welcome change in the attitude of most of the students. Maturing now, and in some cases with marriage on the horizon, they gradually begin to appreciate the significance of discussions about personal relationships or the problems of buying a house and setting up a home. Suddenly there is more genuine participation and what was airily dismissed a year or two ago now finds a not unwilling acceptance.

For the part-time students, the general studies period is one of the few occasions when they have a chance of coming into contact with ideas and controlled discussion of them. It is a gallant attempt to nurture a sense of values, to underline an awareness of our responsibilities towards others, and to reveal, no matter how inadequately, a vision of a richer, fuller life. Despite the uncertainties and the cynicism, there is no doubt at all about the exciting teaching, the stimulating projects, and the fascinating variety of the work being carried out under the aegis of general studies. It has been one of the most significant and encouraging developments in colleges over the last fifteen years.

The third function of many general education departments is providing adult education. Many colleges now share with the Workers' Educational Association (WEA), university extra-mural departments, evening centres, and community schools in organising a programme of recreational and leisure courses, officially called 'non-vocational' courses.

What we do is to group together all the non-vocational courses, such as pottery, cookery, woodwork and car maintenance run by the different departments. Then we appoint some keen young lecturer, strong as an ox and full of missionary zeal, to develop the work. Ideally he should have a wife who does not mind becoming an 'FE widow', with her husband out several nights a week chasing all over the landscape.

Colleges have been running evening classes ever since the nineteenth century but these were mainly technical in nature. There was little attempt to provide anything in the way of leisure or non-vocational courses except for a little bit of cookery and dressmaking. This was considered the province of the evening institute meeting on the premises of the local secondary school.

Most college principals, because of their engineering or science backgrounds, had little time for non-vocational courses. They tended to equate these with the Youth Service as a worthy but quite minor activity and one outside the main-stream of their work. I think you can probably understand this point of view. They were quite happy to leave such trivia to the evening centres which, being part-time institutions, were unworthy of much attention either. As for the more serious intellectual evening pursuits, these were surely the concern of the 'responsible bodies', those earnest souls in the WEA and the university extra-mural departments.

Despite this, a few principals felt that arranging a rich and satisfying programme of leisure classes for adults was as much a function of a college as providing a day-release course in panel-beating for lads in the motor trade. It was also in accord with section 41 of the 1944 Education Act, which charged LEAs with the duty of 'securing the provision of leisure time occupation in such organised cultural training and recreative activities as are suited for their requirements, for any persons over compulsory school age who are able and willing to profit by the facilities provided for that purpose'. If you see what they mean.

These early stirrings were given a boost a few years ago by the emergence of the idea of education for leisure. This delightful title (we are rather good at catchpenny titles in further education) was not exactly brand-new but it suddenly began to be bandied about in high places. Thanks to the spread of automation and other technological miracles, millions of workers in the new Utopia would have long idle hours to while away. Fretwork and morris-dancing being out of fashion, physical recreation and intellectual pursuits would be the order of the day.

Gradually colleges began to provide programmes of non-vocational classes. But it still remained something of a fringe activity until the late 'sixties when the DES declared that adult education was a field all colleges should cultivate.

Principals took the point and there was a welcome spurt of activity—genuinely welcomed because colleges have superb facilities which evening centres cannot possibly match. They can also provide, as long as classrooms and specialist rooms are free, non-vocational classes during the day as well. This is helpful for older people who do not wish to venture out at night and a boon to pensioners some of whom now enjoy classes specially arranged for them.

In certain areas where the geography is favourable some colleges have gone further and, with the approval of their LEA, have set up departments of adult education under a head who is responsible for the organisation of all adult education in the area, both day and evening. This arrangement is simple, cheap, and effective and it does enable sensible provision to be made. For instance, first or first and second year courses may be held at evening centres while the more advanced courses are concentrated in the college. Often the area programme is planned in collaboration with the local secretaries of the 'responsible bodies'. Thus a spirit of harmony and cooperation is engendered and over-lapping avoided.

Such departments are meeting genuine community needs and have now started including in their work the education of adult illiterates, immigrants, hospital patients and the handicapped. This is valuable pioneer work and just as the name 'community college' is beginning to be heard here and there so, too, is 'department of community education'.

Almost certainly you have seen, experienced or read about a strange phenomenon which occurs outside your local college every September. For several evenings in the middle of the month, the college car parks are jammed and vehicles lie nose to tail in all the surrounding streets. All sorts and conditions of men and women converge upon the college; teenagers in old bangers, elderly ladies on bicycles, smart young matrons in the second car, and a flood of assorted pedestrians bear down upon us. For this is the period of enrolment for evening classes—or what is popularly known as 'signing on for night school'.

People will persist in calling it 'night school'. We avoid this expression like the plague because it conjures up visions of the horny-handed labouring over their tables in some cheerless barracks. I thought we had managed to knock this title on the head a few years back, but it seems a long time a-dying.

Long before the official opening time there is a queue outside the main doors and snaking round the building. Pray God it's a fine night! The local press is there in force and pictures of the swarming ratepayers appear at the week-end. The colleges now have their enrolment procedures down to a fine art and they deal expeditiously with hundreds, often thousands, of people in the short space of a few evenings.

I expect you have a shrewd idea of the variety of evening classes your local college provides, ranging from boat-building to beauty culture and from French to fly-fishing. The most impressive list of courses is contained in the ILEA's annual booklet *Floodlight*. This always gets an honourable mention in the national press (and deservedly so) because of the enormous diversity of its classes. In the ILEA you can indulge, if you have the mind for it, in such curious activities as face massage, Hindi, marquetry, pigeons (care and breeding of), verse speaking, or Egyptology.

Yet adult education, although it has expanded tremendously in FE, is always under threat. You see, it is not what we call 'statutory provision', i.e. there is no legal requirement for it to be provided by the LEA, like full-time education up to the age of 16. Cynics in education know that whenever there is an economic crisis (there was one in 1969 and there is another raging as I write in early 1976) the national axe will fall on building programmes and one of the first items the LEA's pruners will turn their attention to is adult education. These days it is one of the few heads of expenditure an education committee can cut without actually damaging the main fabric of education. This is understandable though hard for enthusiasts to swallow. The cost of running evening classes is tiny compared with an LEA's total budget for education, but when education committees up and down the country, in desperate financial straits, are being forced to make all kinds of painful cuts, it becomes a question of priorities and adult education has to bear its share. So once again, no doubt, fees will be increased, the range of classes reduced, and in a few cases adult education provision may be threatened with suspension until sunnier times. It is all rather a pity.

For many older people, attendance at evening classes is one of the few cultural activities they can afford. For thousands of young married women with small children, dressmaking classes provide a chance to make the housekeeping go a little further by learning how to make simple garments. They also offer a brief escape from all-engulfing domesticity. We have been reminded so often in the past about the part that evening centres can play in developing community spirit and in creating a sense of neighbourhood in new towns and new estates that it is sad to see it *in extremis* yet again. Fortunately adult education has proved remarkably resilient over the years and will rise again.

A fourth function exercised by the general education department is to provide physical education and physical recreation throughout the college during the day and in the evening. It is a servicing function like that for English and general studies. In recent years physical education provision in the evenings has mushroomed (paralleling the boom in leisure activities provided commercially) and it is one of the most popular features of any evening centre programme.

Because of the increasing scope of its work, the general education department is now often the largest of the departments in a college. As far as general studies is concerned, a sizeable staff enables the head of department to create a team of varied talents essential for providing an attractive and stimulating programme. The members of the team tend to be people with an arts or social sciences background with wide-ranging interests in literature, music and drama, and in educational ideas and experiments.

Again, many of the departmental staff will have taught in secondary schools and will be used to concepts like pastoral care. They will also have certain attitudes towards extra-curricular activities and their value in college life. Because of the nature of the staff, this department is often regarded as a catalyst in a college.

This is its special importance. From it spring many of the formal and informal activities and societies involving staff and students. Not all, of course, and before I am jumped on, I must stress that this department has no monopoly here. There are plenty of college societies and activities which draw their inspiration from members of staff with quite different backgrounds. Moreover, we all realise that the productions of plays and concerts and the staging of exhibitions would be quite impossible without the efforts of talented teachers from other departments. Yet on balance, I think this picture is a fair one. As I pointed out earlier, one of our problems in colleges is giving the student a sense of belonging, a feeling that he is a member of a community that cares as much about what goes on outside the classroom as it does about what goes on inside. It is here that this department makes its distinctive contribution to the life of a college.

CHAPTER TWELVE

Public relations

A word fitly spoken is like apples of gold in pictures of silver.
Proverbs 25:11

Colleges have to advertise to live. No full-time student is compelled by law to come to us. All such students are volunteers; there are no pressed men. If students did not come forward we should be out of business. As far as the colleges are concerned, there is no truth in the old saying, 'A good wine needs no bush', i.e., a first-rate product needs no advertising. We have a first-rate service to offer, but we have to sell it to the public. So principals and heads of department need to be primed with messianic fervour for one of their main charges is to go forth, preach the word, and multiply the students.

As we have seen, the wealth of opportunities in further education is only now beginning to impinge on the public consciousness despite the achievements of the last fifteen years and the efforts of many bodies to publicise them. Yet ignorance still persists among parents and young people about our full-time courses. Again, the relevance of technical education to our future as a small, highly industrialised nation striving to remain competitive in world markets ought to be blindingly obvious. But, since it isn't, industry has to be told about what we have to offer and encouraged to take advantage of it.

Two things are vital for our public relations. First, a steady stream of accurate and up-to-date information directed from both national and local level at those who need it. Secondly, the colleges must take positive steps to promote cooperation and understanding with the interested parties—employers, schools, parents and the general public. The DES is certainly doing its best with the production of various pamphlets, primarily aimed at telling the schools all about us, but it is difficult to gauge their effect. The colleges in their turn rain literature down upon the schools (leaflets, prospectuses, letters, brochures) because this is where we recruit most of our full-time students.

But we have our problems. The truth is that as far as spreading the gospel goes we are virtually in the hands of the head teachers. If they are hostile to further education then our publicity material gets no further than the wastepaper basket. And the heads sometimes prove a blockage in the pipe of communication.

Let us deal with the grammar schools first. Their pupils are well briefed about universities and colleges of education but they are often woefully ignorant of the career opportunities available in the colleges. Most grammar school head teachers are arts graduates with little knowledge of, or sympathy with, engineering, science and technology. I can find it in my heart to forgive them this, but I cannot forgive them denying young people the chance to profit by the opportunities which exist in FE.

It is important that sixth formers know about the wide range of CNAA and other degree courses available in the technical colleges. Many of them find it impossible to enter the university of their choice, yet every September there are places in degree courses in the technical colleges going begging simply because sixth formers do not know about them. The DES is doing much to help through special publications and its Further Education Information Service but we are still losing far too many bright youngsters for comfort. The schools should not shrug off their responsibilities on to *The Sunday Times*.

It is a truth universally acknowledged that further education is loved by few, and the apathy and occasional hostility of the grammar schools towards technical and further education is regrettable. Our overtures, the winning glances, the hand of friendship are rejected or coolly turned aside.

Fortunately the position is happier with comprehensive and secondary modern schools. Their head teachers are aware of the importance vocational studies are assuming in the schools and are much more sympathetic towards us. So a kind of delicate and tentative partnership is developing. How shall we nourish this tender shoot? Not by saying such hard things about the schools and their attitudes, you will say. *Touché*. But we are all part of the same educational family and plain speaking within the family often has salutary effects.

There are several ways in which colleges seek to win the cooperation and support of the secondary schools in their catchment areas. One of them is involvement. It is useful if head teachers can be persuaded to serve on appropriate advisory committees of the college. Again, in most towns teachers in the schools are friendly with staff at the college, and this can lead to fruitful visits by groups of secondary school teachers and also by parties of pupils. School-parties, in fact, are frequent and welcome visitors either on general occasions like an open day, a play, or an exhibition, or for tours to special parts or particular departments of the college. Boys keen on going into the industry will be interested in seeing the engineering workshops in action and girls thinking of a career in business will enjoy having audio-typing and the latest office machinery demonstrated to them. For many boys and girls this will be their first insight into the world of FE.

'Link' courses also help to bring pupils into more intimate contact with the college. This is the name given to a variety of arrangements under which pupils in their last year at school spend a day or part of a day at their local college.

Colleges have marvellous facilities like computers, brick-work shops, catering kitchens and motor vehicle work-shops. Where there is spare capacity it is sensible to offer it to the schools and to arrange appropriate courses. These provide a useful bridge between the world of school and the world of employment, and serve as an introduction to further education.

Link courses aim at doing ane of two things; enabling a pupil to persue a vocational interest already aroused or providing him with the choice of sampling a range of skills and experiences. Most courses have tended to be practical ones in building and engineering, arranged for the less able pupils, but many colleges are running courses in a variety of subjects leading to GCE and CSE qualifications.

In their short life link courses have met with some success, especially when the school and college have collaborated in designing the course and the school has chosen a group of interested boys and girls to attend it. Some colleges have several hundred 15 year olds attending courses each week and many of them will eventually find their way into full- or part-time courses.

Yet it looks as though link courses may decline as rapidly as they have arisen. Education committees have realised that link courses are expensive in terms of staff costs—they are, in fact, paying twice for tuition at school and at college. A more powerful reason is that most colleges are now full up and, despite a willingness to help, they simply have no spare accommodation for courses which by their nature cannot be high on the list of college priorities.

Finally, principals go out of their way for obvious reasons to establish cordial relations with head teachers. Entertaining, informal meetings, and invitations to college functions all engender a degree of goodwill which helps to demolish the barriers to trust and confidence. These efforts are reinforced by the activities of heads of department visiting schools to talk to school leavers and to discuss new college courses with members of staff.

Trust and confidence built on mutual esteem. Admirable sentiment, worthy objective! Let us hope colleges and schools will strive towards it for the sake of (and we had almost forgotten them) our young people.

There are several things wrong with colleges of FE (I wouldn't like you to feel that we are wholly blameless) and one of them is our attitude, or non-attitude, to parents. A satisfied parent is the best advertisement a college can have

K

but we pay them scant attention. Perhaps this is another legacy from the time when we were dealing primarily with part-time students.

Our attitude must sometimes strike parents of full-time students as rather odd. They have been used to taking their offspring to the local primary school, meeting the head teacher, attending sports days, and coming in regularly to discuss their child's progress with the staff. Later, at the secondary school, relationships between home and school may well have intensified. There will have been exhibitions of works to see and concerts and prize days to attend. Many parents will have been active in parent/teacher associations and will have got to know members of the staff quite well over the years. Then their child opts for further education, disappears into the maw of the college, and vanishes as though into a void. It is true (at least I hope it is true) that the parents will almost certainly meet the head of department or one of his senior staff to discuss their child's future course, but after that—not much.

Gone are the happy days of making costumes for the school play, brewing great pots of tea on sports day, cosy get-togethers with the staff for bring and buy sales, jolly committees raising thousands for a swimming pool—all the innocent and useful activities that schools encourage to strengthen the links between classroom and home. Alas, all are gone.

Now this is not good enough and the colleges could well take a leaf out of the schools' book here. There is a fund of goodwill among parents towards any institution and its teachers that educate their children. But that goodwill requires periodic nourishment and reassurance. If a parent is committing his child to a college for one to three years, he will feel infinitely more comfortable for an occasional sight of the inside and for the chance of a chat with 'old Jacko', or 'that Miss Jones', or 'Nobby'—creatures otherwise of some academic never-never land. It is salutary to see the eagerness with which parents jump at any chance of viewing the mysteries of the college and meeting the staff, and their delight in being invited to do so.

It is gratifying to see that more colleges are now organising parents' evenings and are taking such opportunities as open days, exhibitions, and college plays to involve parents in their local college.

I mentioned open days because this is one way in which our colleges of FE can bring home to the public what they have to offer. Open days involve a great deal of hard work and the rewards are intangible, but they should be seen as part of the college pattern of publicity, the effect of which is cumulative. If it is not always possible to demonstrate the higher academic work, we can usually give a good idea of the range and quality of the theoretical and practical work, and it does satisfy the curiosity of thousands of ratepayers and parents about the facilities for science and technology they have only vaguely heard about. If principals do not open their colleges and stimulate interest in their work they can hardly complain of lack of public interest and support at times of crisis.

You are probably unaware how much our halls, lecture theatres, sports halls, and committee rooms are used by outside organisations for conferences, exhibitions, meetings, and displays. We welcome these non-college functions because it is all useful publicity and it attracts potential customers. We are usually at our best on these occasions and visitors are invariably impressed—as indeed they should be.

There has been a medley mixture using my premises this year. We have had the local Astronomical Society, the Chester Film Society, the Institute of Clerks of Works, Post Office Electrical Engineers, the National Esperanto Conference, a conference for our own regional electricity board, part of the local Arts Festival, a play performed by the Young Farmers, and meetings of many other bodies. All is grist to our mill and excellent public relations it makes too.

The college conveys its message to the public through its prospectus and its leaflets. Prospectuses have become something of a status symbol. For years they were terrible: poorly designed, badly laid out, and conveying the maximum of information with the minimum of clarity. Too often they were printed, like Browning's scrofulous French novel, 'on grey paper with blunt type'.

They have recently undergone a transformation. The cry for less matter with more art has been heeded and colleges now compete in producing glossies that compare favourably with anything that industry puts out. And why not, indeed? Many colleges have their own schools or departments of art so there is really no need for the principal to exercise his lack of taste upon the college's major publication. The new-style prospectuses are good for the image, even though some look as if they cost a small fortune to produce.

Leaflets, too, are equally gay and arresting instead of looking like a local handout for a sale of damaged carpets. For effective communication with the public, this high standard of design should be echoed throughout all the college's printed matter. Headed paper, leaflets, postcards, even compliment slips, all these should have an individual flavour, a house style that stamps the college firmly and colourfully on the public mind. Since many colleges have departments of both art and business studies what they send out should reflect the flair and design skills of the former reinforced by the pungency and efficiency of the latter.

This flood of information descends upon our friends in industry and business as well as upon our colleagues in the schools. Industry and business have some trouble in keeping up-to-date with the details of our day-release and block-release courses, especially in engineering and building. You can hardly blame them for this. We can barely keep abreast of the rapid changes ourselves. Although the college blankets firms in its area with publicity material, it is still the responsibility of the head of department to go out and make sure that firms are kept fully informed about what his department has to offer.

How do we seek to strengthen the bonds between the college and industry and commerce? I have already referred to the valuable part played by the advisory committees and by truly representative governing bodies. Some authorities, in association with the former Ministry of Technology, appointed industrial liaison officers with a remit to make the industries and organisations in their areas aware of the range of facilities available in colleges and elsewhere and to promote the use of them. But in most colleges the responsibility for making friends and influencing people lies with the principal, heads of department, and the senior staff. The head of department again sets an example here, as in other directions, by assiduous visiting of major customers, by involving such firms in the work of his department, and by establishing cordial relations with his opposite numbers. Like the liaison officer, only by constant contact with industry can he identify needs over and above the standard pattern of courses, and meet these by courses specially tailored to his customers' requirements.

One short cut to cordiality, by the way, is a meal in the training restaurant of the hotel and catering department. Here the food and service is usually first-class and visitors visibly warm towards you.

All but the most junior members of staff should be encouraged to go out visiting as part of their normal work. They need to see new processes, keep up-to-date with recent developments in their own field, establish personal contact at appropriate levels, visit their students while they are at work and discuss any problems with the training officer or supervisor. Some large colleges may have between 500 and 1,000 firms contributing students, so public relations is something which nearly all the staff must share. I do not think that teachers in our colleges quite realise the magnitude of the task or fully appreciate its importance. Their horizon can no longer be limited by the classroom, workshop or laboratory. By opting to serve in further education they have entered an extra dimension.

The responsibility for public relations rests with the principal. In a large college he will delegate some of this but, delegate as he may, all principals bear the lion's share of the work. They devote considerable time to visiting schools, serving on local committees, attending prize-givings at local firms and hospitals, eating official dinners given by bodies associated with the colleges, talking about further education to all kinds of organisations, calling on firms, and entertaining a stream of variegated visitors. This plays havoc with their private life (do principals have any private life?) and they have to strike a sensible balance between this side of their work and the management of the college proper. But no principal can escape from the responsibility of projecting an image of FE and of his own college which will win the respect of industry and gain the confidence of parents.

Let the watchword of a college of FE be F for friendly and E for efficient. It is no good being the first without the second, and the second, although admirable in its way, is by itself a little too clinical for comfort. But if a college can be both F and E, well then . . .

We cannot leave public relations without mentioning the newspapers. Although further education still rarely makes the national headlines, we figure prominently on our own patch. The local press are good friends of FE and hardly a week goes by without some picture or paragraph about the college appearing in the local papers. The college is the largest educational institution in sight and our multifarious activities appeal to the cub reporter hungry for copy. When a reporter is desperate, the tech is usually good for some titbit especially if the general studies people have been carrying out another of their surveys about pre-marital sex. One enterprising colleague of mine even contributes a regular weekly column about college activities to his local paper. Gentlemen of the press, we salute you!

CHAPTER THIRTEEN

How it all began . . .

I wore clean collars and a brand new suit
For the pass examination at the Institute.
                                        HMS Pinafore W. S. Gilbert

All too often books of this kind begin with an historical chapter, prefaced by a plea that in order to understand what is happening now it is important to grasp what has gone before. This is all very well but I felt you might find it rather off-putting to be faced with such a chapter when you were drawing away from the kerb so to speak. Therefore I have deliberately placed my potted history towards the end. I am assuming that if anyone has had the patience and stamina to wade through this far, then his moral fibre is now sufficiently toughened to take an historical review in its stride. If, however, you feel that such a chapter is irrelevant, obtrusive, or, even worse, a bore, then pass swiftly on.

But I hope you will linger. I enjoyed writing this chapter. I found it refreshing to drop my anchor on a bottom of hard fact after being afloat for several chapters on a sea of speculation. And since there is no readily-available, brief account of the development of technical education in England I am vain enough to hope that this little chapter may be useful.

How did it all begin? For centuries before the industrial revolution craft training had been the province of the mediaeval guilds. The mysteries of the various crafts were passed on from master to apprentice by the method we call today 'sitting next to Nellie'. And this was sufficient until the industrial revolution and the growth of the factory system. The making of goods by hand began to be replaced by the making of goods by machinery and many workers became adjusters and supervisors of machines. There arose a hunger among adults for instruction, not only in the three Rs, but for instruction in the principles underlying workshop practice. This is why the early history of technical education in England is so entwined with adult education and with elementary and scientific education, constantly overlapping and with no fixed boundaries, the threads tangled, the pattern confused.

This desire for technical education was apparent at both ends of the social scale. Cultivated men, despairing of any contribution from the ancient universities and stirred by the industrial revolution in England and the social revolution in France, founded their own institutions like the Warrington Academy and Anderson's Institution (1796), which later became the Royal College of Science and Technology. It is easy to joke about Warrington with its Rugby League, beer, bingo and aroma of soap flakes, but its Academy had an international scientific reputation at the end of the eighteenth century and its lecturers had a great influence on educational development in the north-west. One of them for a while was none other than Marat, the French Revolutionary leader, though what he made of it I do not know. The Academy is still there—just. It stands desolate, decaying, riddled with dry rot. Go and pay your respects before it falls down.

One of the early professors at Anderson's Institution was George Birkbeck. He started classes for working men and intelligent artisans who wished to gain some knowledge of the scientific principles underlying their crafts. These classes were the seed of the Mechanics Institute movement. George Birkbeck moved to London and in 1823 he founded a Mechanics Institution there—which eventually became Birkbeck College. This was so successful that many large industrial cities like Manchester, Bradford, Birmingham and Sheffield soon followed suit. Although the middle class founders of these institutes had various motives, what attracted thousands of working men was simply the opportunity for self-improvement. So rapid was the development that by 1850 there were well over six hundred Institutes with a membership of over half a million.

Art was given an important place in the Mechanics Institutes because of its relation to industrial design. In addition, following the report of a Select Committee on Arts and Manufacturers in 1835, the Government set up special Schools of Design in London and the provinces. The School of Design in London eventually became the Royal College of Art while the seventeen provincial schools, developing for the most part independently of the Mechanics Institutes, were eventually absorbed into the national system of technical education.

The Mechanics Institutes' buildings usually included a library, a reading room, and a room for debates and lectures. For a picture of one of these embryo institutions let us turn to Samuel Smiles. You may sneer at *Self Help* but read it; you can hardly fail to be stirred. Writing in 1859, Smiles gives a vivid account of the origins of a Mechanics Institute which he visited in the north in 1844: 'It was started by two or three young men of the humblest rank who resolved to meet in the winter evenings for the purpose of improving themselves by exchanging knowledge with each other. Their first meetings were held in a room of a cottage in which one of the members lived; but as others shortly joined them, the place soon became inconveniently full. Though they were for the most part young men earning comparatively small weekly wages, they resolved to incur the risk of hiring a room; and, on making enquiry, they found a large dingy apartment to let, which had been used as a temporary Cholera Hospital. No tenant could be found for the place which was avoided as if the plague still clung to it. But the mutual improvement youths, nothing daunted, hired the cholera room at so much a week, lit it up, placed a few benches and a deal table in it, and began their winter classes'. One feels that this is technical education in a nutshell. 'Self Help' is very apt. It might almost be the slogan for education in this part of the century.

The dramatic growth of the Mechanics Institutes reflected this desire among the working class for simple technical education—for education of any sort, in fact. It is difficult for us to realise that at this time there was no national system of education. Elementary education for children was provided by the Church of England and other religious bodies but working men had to seize instruction wherever it was

offered. This was often in the night schools run by men like
Bartle Massey, the lame schoolmaster, so movingly described by George Eliot in *Adam Bede*. Most of these night
schools were held in day school premises and the majority
were run as private ventures by day school teachers. The
chief supporters were artisans and factory hands paying an
admission charge of 1d per week and upwards.

The work of the Mechanics Institutes, however, was
hampered from the start by the lack of basic education
among its members. This was one of the fatal flaws that led
to the movement withering away. Another was that the
original programmes, with their preoccupation with science,
were a little too ambitious for even the skilled working men
the Institutes hoped to attract. Thus they rapidly lost contact
with their primary audience and most Institutes subsided
into middle class organisations offering lectures of general
scientific and literary interest.

A further blow was struck by the Public Libraries Act of
1850. Libraries were an attractive feature of the early Institutes. Where else in a growing industrial town was there
access to a collection of books even remotely technical in
nature—or access to books of any kind? The establishment
of public libraries meant that information previously only
available in the Mechanics Institute was now much more
accessible and in a more up-to-date form. In some cases the
new libraries took over the existing collection in the Institutes.

We are so used to the idea today that economic and technological progress can only be made if it is backed up by an
adequate system of technical education, that it is remarkable
to see the Victorian industrial juggernaut plunging inexorably forward without it. Manufacturers saw little point in
providing anything other than training in workshop practice.
Since theory could not be taught in a factory, they felt this
was the responsibility of other agencies. Hence arose that
unhappy division between training and education which has
bedevilled technical education ever since.

Then in 1851 there occurred a phenomenon that was to
have a profound effect upon the course of technical

education. This was not apparent at the time but hindsight makes it a watershed in our educational history. The Great Exhibition in Hyde Park, a breath-taking display of art and crafts and manufactures, had the same galvanising effect on education in England that the Russian Sputnik had on mathematical and scientific education in the United States after 1957. It opened the eyes of many to the industrial progress being made in Europe and a few prophets connected this with their systems of education. Gradually we became aware that England herself, at the high noon of her industrial supremacy and sophistication, might well lose this position unless she established an underpinning of education. In fact, this is what did happen. Germany and the United States, although late into the field, made such rapid progress that by 1900 they had overhauled us in industrial capacity. And we, lulled by the languor of the long Edwardian afternoon, failed to realise this—until Ypres.

After 1851 there was a growing realisation that a country dependent upon the skills of its workforce in an increasingly competitive age could no longer tolerate a so-called educational system in which most working people received little or no schooling, and which left technical education to voluntary effort. At this time technical education provision was still restricted to Mechanics Institutes and the more advanced night schools. Although the Mechanics Institutes began to decline in importance during the second half of the century, the period 1850–1890 saw, both in London and the provinces, a swift, if uncoordinated, expansion of technical education in other forms, at differing levels, and under various auspices. But provision firmly remained evening-based.

The main impetus in technical education after the Great Exhibition was the newly created Department of Science and Art whose primary aim was the promotion of the applied sciences. From 1859 it fostered this cause by making grants to establish 'science' classes and by setting up an annual examination system under which teachers received a bonus according to their results—the famous 'payment by results' scheme. Scrupulously avoiding teaching crafts or trades, the classes tended to be largely theoretical in content. How theoretical even the practical classes could get is illustrated in H. G. Wells', *The New Machiavelli*. The author is describing his father who was one of the early teachers:

'He did not do experiments if he could possibly help it because in the first place they used up gas for the Bunsen Burner and good material in ruinous fashion, and in the second they were, in his rather careless and sketchy way, apt to endanger the apparatus of the institute and even the lives of his students. Then thirdly, real experiments involved washing up . . . He had a preference for what he called an illustrative experiment; which was simply an arrangement of the apparatus in front of the class with nothing whatever by way of material, and then a slow luminous description of just what you did put in it when you were so ill-advised as to carry the affair beyond illustration, and just exactly what ought to happen when you did'.

During this period an important contribution was made to a rather tangled skein by the examining bodies.

The Royal Society of Arts, for example, was originally founded in 1754 for 'the encouragement of Arts, Manufacture and Commerce'. After its foundation it appears to have rested for a hundred years before suddenly springing into life in 1852. It formed a national union of mechanics institutions and from 1856 it began to organise examinations in science and commerce, although after 1882 it concentrated on commercial subjects. It was thus following in the footsteps of one of the most venerable of the present regional examining unions, the Union of Lancashire and Cheshire Institutes—a title as famous as Manchester United in the north-west but quite unintelligible elsewhere. The Union of Lancashire and Cheshire Institutes was started in 1839 as a union of mechanics institutes. It was not the first because that proud title belongs to the West Riding, but both these unions developed into regional examining bodies over the years, working very closely with that best known body of all, the City and Guilds of London Institute.

The Companies of the City of London feeling, like so many other private and public bodies the need to raise the standard of technical education, started making grants for this purpose in 1869. In 1878 the City and Guilds of London Institute for the Advancement of Technical Education was founded with the aim 'of educating young artisans and others in the scientific and artistic branches of their trades'. The City and Guilds, as they are usually called, forged ahead and established courses of study and examinations for a wide variety of crafts. Now they are the nationally recognised body for craft and technician examinations ranging over some three hundred subjects and they wield much influence, usually for good, throughout the world of technical education, both at home and overseas. Their special value is that they provide a means whereby industries can develop and adopt, on a national basis, schemes of further education which are integral parts of apprenticeship and training programmes.

The City and Guilds also had a teaching function. It started its own institution in 1885 which eventually became one of the three constituent colleges of the Imperial College of Science and Technology. It also founded the Finchley Technical College to provide day and evening courses in science and engineering and Finchley became a model for the technical colleges of the future. The opportunity to study technical subjects during the day was something of a novelty. This was the beginning proper of our system of day-release although its origins can be traced to the early Factory Acts and works schools. It is interesting to note that Finchley, accepting the now traditional view, continued to concentrate on teaching theory and principles with little emphasis on workshop practice.

Meanwhile, you may ask, what had happened to the Mechanics Institutes? These continued to flourish after 1850, reaching the height of their success about 1860, but, as we have seen, the seeds of their decline were already present. Moreover, the Mechanics Institutes, which for years had performed various functions such as technical and art education, continued elementary education, and library provision, found these more and more assumed by the local authorities. In many cases, the new county and county borough councils simply took over the work and premises of the Institutes and this was the origin of many of our oldest technical colleges and technological universities. The rump of the Institutes lingered on into the twentieth century, acting mainly as social clubs, before slowly disappearing. They were the progenitors of technical education and they left behind them a splendid legacy.

In 1867 there was another important exhibition, this time in Paris. The concern that had been voiced by a few in 1851 about the slow progress of technical education in England became more general as a result of the poor showing of the British exhibits there, and disenchantment gave a fresh stimulus to the development of a state system. The establishment of a Select Committee and two Royal Commissions led to Lord Salisbury's government passing the Technical Instruction Act in 1889. This empowered the recently formed county councils to raise a penny rate to promote 'technical and manual instruction' by founding schools and making grants to existing bodies. This expenditure of public funds on technical education, exercised by Technical Instruction Committees, marks the beginning of local as opposed to national responsibility for FE. Once again it was expressly stated that the curriculum should not include the practice of any trade or industry. This attitude contrasts sharply with that on the Continent where the importance of workshop practice in similar schools was emphasised.

If you think that all this is rather gritty, be of good cheer because we are now approaching the congenial period of 'whisky money'. The 1889 Act was really a very modest beginning. A year later, however, there came a sudden windfall in the shape of surplus funds from the Customs and Excise Duties, originally intended to compensate publicans who had lost their licenses under the government's plan to reduce the number of public houses. The government made this whisky money, as the wags called it, over to the county councils to spend on technical education. These two measures gave an impetus to the growth of technical education as intoxicating as Forster's Act of 1870 had given to elementary education.

There was a rush of blood to the head and to build new colleges. A number of splendid buildings in best Accrington brick went up in key centres in Lancashire, and Yorkshire and the south followed suit. Many of these—Burnley is a good example—with their stained glass windows featuring allegorical figures of industry and science (female, over-bosomed, underclad, wearing helmets), their imposing porticos, and their splendid tiles, reflect the pride and confidence of the local citizens in a vision of a kind of education that did not come to pass for another sixty years. But by 1902, when the whisky money ran out, the country's system of technical education was well under way.

This spate of new buildings was accompanied by the rise of the polytechnics. The original polytechnic in Regent Street was founded by Quintin Hogg in 1882. This was so successful that others were established in London under the City Parochial Charities Act of 1883: Battersea, Chelsea, Northern, and Borough in London and the Sir John Cass College and the Northampton Polytechnic in the City itself. Their courses ranged from trade classes to postgraduate work and within a few years they became the most important institutions providing education for industry.

With all this happening much was expected from the Education Act of 1902. This set up local education authorities and gave them responsibility not only for primary and secondary education but also for higher and technical education. But it soon became obvious that the main emphasis was to be placed on developing the secondary sector through the new grammar schools and improving the old elementary schools and that there was going to be precious little left over for technical education. Yet there were two developments.

The Act gave a further fillip to the expansion of the evening continuation schools (later to be called evening institutes) which had grown up rapidly during the 'nineties, and, more important, it led to the establishment of senior and junior technical schools. The latter were not really secondary schools but rather schools designed to fill the gap between the school leaving age and the age of apprenticeship (16) by providing an education for boys wishing to enter a particular industry, usually engineering. They offered a fairly narrow technical curriculum revolving round mathematics, science and drawing with some workshop practice. Many of the 'JTSs' as they came to be called were organised as part of the larger existing senior technical schools and technical colleges, sharing their premises and using their staff. Other JTSs had their own buildings and ran their own evening classes (the headmaster of the JTS was in charge of the evening institute) and in the fullness of time evolved into technical colleges and colleges of further education. They were never very numerous, thanks to our national prejudice against vocational education, and there are none left now but they made a powerful contribution to technical education. They tended to serve a small, well-defined area and for years they turned out a stream of competent and steady lads who found ready employment in local industry. Most of these boys attended evening classes after they left and eventually became the skilled craftsmen, foremen, works managers and in some cases the directors of local firms.

This led to a close relationship between the schools and industry. I imagine that some of you reading this chapter will be products of these very schools and you have every reason to be proud of them. If you detect a sudden note of fervour in my prose you are right. I was personally involved in JTSs. I was not, I hasten to add, involved with the 1902 Education Act and there is no truth in the rumour I was held up to see the old Queen go by. But it so happens that when I became principal of Newton-le-Willows College of Further Education I also became headmaster of the junior technical school attached to it. It had ninety-six boys who came for a two-year course at 13-plus and I arrived just in time to preside over its closure. Over the entrance to the building were incised the words 'Junior Technical School' and even in the 'sixties many traces of former splendour still remained. There were iron-framed desks with oak seats to hold four small boys, fixed science benches of unbelievable solidity, and a curriculum unchanged since 1919—happy days!

The early years of the century also saw some development in day-release with apprentices being allowed time off during the day to attend part-time courses at technical schools and colleges. But the full-time courses at these establishments continued to attract relatively few students.

Much was expected from Fisher's Education Act of 1918. Strange how war focuses attention on education and triggers off advances; it did so again in 1944. This measure sought to raise the school leaving age to 15 and to make attendance at continuation schools for one day per week compulsory for all young people between the ages of 14 and 18. This was nearly sixty years ago! The school leaving age was not raised to 15 until 1947 and compulsory day-release until 18 seems as far off as ever. It is little wonder that Fisher's far-sighted Act met with scant success. As soon as amendments made attendance at a continuation school voluntary, his scheme collapsed and only one authority (Rugby) implemented it.

Thus, soon after the First World War an unhappy pattern of technical education established itself, very different from the hopes and aspirations aroused by the progress of the 'nineties. It was predominantly part-time in character, and although the number of day-release students did increase somewhat, too few firms were either far-sighted enough to realise the value of a trained labour force or sufficiently generous to give their young employees time off during the day to attend the local college. Evening classes ('night school') held in technical institutions crystallised as the only real opportunity for technical education for ambitious boys in engineering and building.

The pattern was consolidated by the introduction in 1921 of the national certificate system. This was a significant step because for the first time professional institutions, the Board of Education, and the colleges became involved in providing a relatively high qualification, through part-time study, for engineers working in industry. There were two levels: ordinary national and higher national. Ordinary national certificate took three years and higher national certificate two years. For full-time students there were similar courses known as diploma courses but these tended to be few and far between. The first scheme for a national certificate in mechanical engineering was followed by others in chemistry, naval architecture, and electrical engineering and later on by ones in building, commerce, textiles, and civil and production engineering. These certificates gave a truly national technical qualification and one that included both theory and practice.

For most students 'getting their national' meant grinding away three evenings a week, not merely for three years but often for four or five because many found themselves unable to pass the various stages at the first attempt. And if they obtained their national, there was, for the able and ambitious, the lure of the higher national, and another two or sometimes three years of further part-time study. This was a long, hard road to professional status but it was a road that thousands successfully travelled for forty years even though it made young men old before their time. In recent years the natural desire of the professional institutions to raise the status of the engineer in England, the increasing complexity and specialisation in the industry, plus the availability of full-time degree courses, has led to this part-time route being virtually closed.

The national certificate system remained the corner-stone of technical education between the Wars. Elsewhere progress was slow. The industrial situation in the 1930s was hardly conducive to the extension of day-release and for most youngsters in industry evening classes in mathematics, science and drawing were still their only salvation. It is salutary and embarrassing to realise that even as recently as 1937/1938 there were only some 20,000 full-time and some 89,000 part-time students in further education. You may feel this is some advance on the meagre figures of thirty years before but the numbers bore little relation to the paramount importance of industry, the size of the work force, and the need for training. Not that industry was particularly training-conscious at that time, or at any time, until it was finally and rudely brought face to face with reality by the Industrial Training Act. Industrial progress and technical education are inextricably interwoven. A prosperous and developing economy requires a vigorous and responsive base of technological education.

There was little building after 1918 until the late 'thirties when several new colleges appeared. They were designed, naturally enough, to fit in with the post-war technical pattern. By day they were used by junior technical schools or junior commercial schools and for part-time day classes, and in the evenings as 'night schools'. But help was on its way.

Butler's 1944 Education Act was responsible for the tripartite system and the creation of technical high schools although few of these were developed. The JTSs continued for a while but were gradually absorbed into the bilateral and comprehensive schools and had almost disappeared by the early 'sixties.

The Act, however, did have far-reaching effects on further education. Until 1944 local education authorities had had the power to provide technical education as part of higher education but, as you might expect, some exercised it more than others. Encouraging noises were obviously not enough and for the first time a statutory duty was imposed on local education authorities, as follows: 'It shall be the duty of every local education authority to secure the provision for their area of adequate facilities for further education, that is to say, full-time and part-time education for persons over compulsory school age'.

This should have been the green light, but as far as further education was concerned, the lights obstinately remained at amber in the immediate post-war years. The government's first duty through the new Ministry of Education was to repair the ravages of the war, and money and effort were directed towards a massive programme of primary and secondary school building. Even so there was a striking increase in the number of students being given day-release. By 1955 there were nearly five times as many day-release students in attendance as there were in 1938 and the number of full-time students had more than trebled. This put a tremendous strain on accommodation. There were few colleges which did not have a variety of 'annexes'. Church halls, huts, old schools, even warehouses and crypts were pressed into service in an effort to cope with the demand. Insanitary and unwholesome annexes are one of the recognised ways of getting new premises. A wily principal always tries to keep

L

some obnoxious building up his sleeve—you never know when it may come in useful as a debating point or a bargaining counter. At last, however, it was the turn of further education and the boom period of technical college expansion started with the title of 'College of Further Education' beginning to impinge upon a baffled public.

Once more came a widespread demand for technical education and, spurred on by the Government White Paper of 1956, expansion continued unabated. Again there came one of our periodic outbursts when those in power are startled into activity by an overwhelming consciousness of the need to make proper provision for technical education. There was, I think, as in the period after 1870, a sudden national concern that unless we quickly geared our technical education to the needs of the post-war world then we should be outstripped in a fiercely competitive battle for world markets. In a few swift years the ugly duckling of the 'thirties was metamorphosed into the glamorous swan of the 'fifties.

In 1957 we had certain large technical colleges designated as colleges of advanced technology (CATS) for advanced and postgraduate work and research; they subsequently became technological universities and left the fold. In 1961 another Government White Paper, *Better Opportunities in Further Education*, attempted to relate our courses more closely to the needs of industry. It introduced technician courses, revisions to the ordinary national certificate courses, a new scheme of craft courses and other reforms and refinements. As we saw earlier, the technician courses and national certificate scheme are now being extensively remodelled by TEC.

The combined effect of the White Papers of 1956 and 1961 was to kill off 'night school' with all its unsavoury implications. The steady increase in day-release enabled the traditional structure of evening classes to be dismantled thus ending the most enduring and unattractive feature of technical education.

During the early 'sixties it seemed that the demands for full-time higher education within FE would increase by leaps and bounds for as far ahead as anyone cared to look. At the same time there was an obvious need in the interests of both economy and efficiency to concentrate these courses in large institutions. The government therefore decided to develop and extend higher education in the technical colleges alongside the universities—this became known as the binary system.

In the 1966 White Paper, *A Plan for Polytechnics and other Colleges*, about seventy major colleges of technology, art and commerce were picked by the DES to form thirty polytechnics in strategic parts of the country 'as the main centres for the future development of full-time higher education within the further education system'. The new polytechnics were intended to complement the universities and colleges of education and the government looked to the chosen few for 'an equally distinguished and separate contribution'.

Like the colleges from which they sprang, the polytechnics are closely linked, in spirit and in function, to the world of industry, business and the professions. As comprehensive institutions, they cater for students studying at every level of higher education. In addition to students reading for CNAA and London University external degrees (including postgraduate and research degrees) and for professional qualifications of degree standard, there are students working for HNDs and other qualifications of sub-degree level. As well as their population of full-time and sandwich students, the polytechnics have many young men and women who are already in employment following advanced courses as part-time students, and there are also all kinds of senior executives and technologists taking management and refresher courses.

One more major upheaval, the effects of which are far from clear at the moment, needs to be recorded. In 1973, the DES, alarmed at the over-production of teachers, decided to cut back the number of training places in colleges of education. It proposed to use the spare capacity to diversify their work and also, by linking certain colleges with nearby FE ones to form new high-level (but non-polytechnic) institutions. As I write, over twenty large FE colleges are busy amalgamating with colleges of education.

This is another example of the way in which, since the war, FE has generated a stream of high-level institutions based on need and demand, only to see the structure decapitated. We have seen our colleges transmogrified into CATS (1957), into polytechnics (1966), and now into these hybrids. FE is like the dreaded Hydra; so vigorous and resilient is it that no sooner do you cut off its head than another grows in its place.

During the last decade a spate of White Papers and reports, a torrent of bulletins and memoranda, have continued to pour down upon our inoffensive heads. Committees have been set up to look into this and advise upon that; recommendations and reports have landed on our desks with sickening thumps at ever-decreasing intervals. I suppose this is a small price to pay for what has been called the 'FE explosion'. This is a worn-out phrase now but it aptly describes the huge increase in demand at all levels, especially for full-time courses, and the immense sums spent on buildings and equipment to match it.

The latest provisional figures (1974) show that there are over 335,000 full-time and 727,000 part-time day students in FE compared with 52,000 and 333,000 respectively in 1953. Today the country is aware as never before of the need for further education and our brick and glass palaces, throbbing by day and glowing by night, stand glittering witnesses to the vision of the early pioneers.

CHAPTER FOURTEEN

Problems and perspectives

In a contemplative fashion,
  And a tranquil frame of mind,
Free from every kind of passion
  Some solution let us find.

The Gondoliers W. S. Gilbert

So there it is. The wheel has come full circle and our journey is almost over. I suppose the most irritating thing about writing a book on FE is the speed with which it becomes out-of-date. My book was first written in 1969 and, in revising it, I have been embarrassed by the scale and variety of the alterations I have had to make. I have corrected it as best I can but if odd passages still strike you as faintly out-of-date you must put it down to the whirlygig of time—or my inadequacy.

At least I hope I have given you some insight into what goes on behind the walls of your local college of FE and have conveyed something of the variety of our students and teachers, and a little of their activities, academic and otherwise. I also hope I have aroused some sympathy for our aims and aspirations so that we shall no longer remain the forgotten sector of education.

Before I leave you, I thought it might be helpful to essay a glimpse into the future (a future which I think is clearer now than it was in 1969) and to look briefly at one or two problems facing the FE sector.

Actually individual FE colleges have few real problems, although the FE sector itself has several. That is a rash comment, and if it sounds slightly contradictory, let me expand it a little. Certainly FE is strapped for cash at present and is likely to be underprivileged for several years, but it shares this with the rest of the education service.

But at least we are free from certain problems which affect other sectors. We do not have the disciplinary problems which are plaguing some comprehensive schools in urban areas. We are not experiencing the traumatic reorganisation which is shaking the colleges of education. And we do not share the difficulties of many polytechnics and some university departments in attracting adequate numbers of qualified students into our courses. Our major problem stems from the fact that FE, now seen as the success story of post-war education, has, in fact, been too successful for its own good. We are currently attracting full-time students in such numbers that many colleges of FE have little space to spare while several are facing an acute accommodation crisis.

How has this suddenly come about? As we saw earlier, during the last fifteen years there has been a great increase in the range of full-time courses in FE and today one-third of all students aged 16-19 in full-time education are in FE colleges. Part of this massive expansion is accounted for by the thousands of students taking orthodox GCE A and O level courses, of which a little more in a moment. Then the raising of the school leaving age to 16 gave a further stimulus to the movement for a longer educational life. And of those staying on, more and more are opting for various reasons to take either academic or vocational courses in FE.

But there is more to it than this. FE has always been proud of its reputation to identify need and meet it rapidly, to respond quickly to demand, whether local or national. We have been proud of our flexibility and the range of expertise available among our staff. No wonder we boast that we can grow hair on billiard balls. So in recent years, in addition to our traditional pattern of full-time and part-time vocational courses and our general education work, we have become involved in providing premises and preliminary courses for the Open University, facilities and courses for numerous training boards, TOPS courses for the Training Services Agency, adult education, link courses for the schools, and in 1975 many of us took the Adult Literacy scheme under our wing.

Then in the autumn of that year we were faced with a huge influx of full-time students mainly because of the employment position. Not only did we cater for them but we also provided all kinds of courses at very short notice under difficult conditions for many unemployed school leavers.

As a result of our readiness to meet demands of all kinds at all levels we have now virtually destroyed our ability to respond. Some of us can take no more students and many of us have no more money to finance new work. We shall soon be in the unhappy position of having to turn students away for the first time in our history.

What we have seen in a few brief years is, in essence, the sudden emergence of a new role for FE colleges. It will take some time for us to adjust to this and to realise that our accustomed patterns are dissolving rapidly around us. I mentioned earlier the idea of community colleges, the title underlining the concept of the local college meeting community needs at different levels. Of course, colleges have always done this in engineering, science, and commerce and more recently in general and adult education. What we are seeing now is an identification of FE with a much wider sector of the community. On top of the work we have assumed in the last few years, FE is also being asked to provide for the educational needs of the disadvantaged (socially or academically), the handicapped (mentally or physically), 'ethnic minority groups', pensioners, the unemployed, old people in residential homes, and patients in various types of hospital.

Central government, is also showing concern for those young people who leave school to enter employment which gives little systematic training and no further education. The DES and the TSA are planning to introduce short, experimental courses of what is termed 'vocational preparation', combining education and training, in an attempt to provide more satisfactorily for this large and hitherto neglected group of young people. Inevitably most of this work will be done by the colleges.

Central government, organisations and individuals keep turning to FE because FE cares and because FE can cope. Yet we are bound to ask how many more burdens FE can assume. It is ironic that all these pressures and demands upon us have arisen within a very short space of time and at the one moment historically when FE is ill-equipped to help. If we are to respond as the community, the LEAs and Westminster wish us to respond, then we hope we shall enjoy the resources to do so—and this means accommodation and money to pay for the extra staff and equipment needed.

There are three major problems affecting the FE sector. Some problems steal up and overwhelm you unobserved. One moment they seem a small cloud on the horizon no bigger than a man's hand; the next, storm clouds fill the skies. This is the case with provision for the 16–19 age group and the problem of reconciling what should be provided in colleges with what should be provided in the sixth forms of schools of various types. Although FE has sounded the alarm for over fifteen years, it is only in the last couple of years, when the harsh economic situation has suddenly and painfully brought the problem into focus, that our warnings have been heeded by administrators and elected members.

Present provision for the 16–19s is a jungle, a series of casual growths which have been allowed to take place un-checked and unplanned. We now have two systems (a minor binary set-up) existing uneasily side by side: the secondary schools operating under secondary regulations and the colleges of further education catering for the same age group under quite different regulations.

As a result we find comprehensive schools, sixth form colleges, grammar schools, tertiary colleges, and FE colleges, all engaged in wooing the sixth former. Not a very happy picture, and one offering every incitement to rivalry, tension, and waste. It is good to be able to offer a choice between school and college after 16, but one wonders how long we can afford to continue to do so.

Ten years ago the problem appeared to be that of resolv-ing what was mistakenly interpreted as the duplication of A level courses in schools and colleges. Today, with FE firmly established as a major provider of both general and vocational education, the problem has changed its nature. Highlighted by the economic crisis, the emphasis is on the need to rationalise and unify the structure of post-16 education to provide a pattern of full-time education relevant to the social and individual needs of this age group.

As a result of attempts to do this, two types of post-16 institutions have emerged over the last few years—sixth form colleges and tertiary colleges. The fundamental difference between them is that the latter provide both full-time and part-time courses for young people over 16. These colleges have developed from FE colleges, nearly all of which of course are tertiary in character.

More numerous at the moment than tertiary colleges are the sixth form colleges. These are institutions fed by non-selective schools and they reflect the new, broadened sixth form in their provision of academic courses and, occasionally, vocationally-biased courses on a full-time basis. I cannot help thinking, in view of recent social and educational developments, that sixth form colleges are unlikely to provide a model for the future.

Many LEAs, reeling under the combined impact of inflation and massive cuts in government spending on education, are looking carefully at various ways of re-organising 16–19 provision on cheaper and more effective lines. This is not so easy in areas where reorganisation on comprehensive lines is complete, but in those areas where there is room for manoeuvre, some LEAs (Oxfordshire and Staffordshire, for example) are making a careful assessment of the resources available for the 16–19s in their schools and colleges and trying to make sensible provision for this demanding, difficult, and expensive group of young people.

But is it too late? With these new ideas and the increasing popularity of FE among the 16 year olds who wish to continue in full-time education, we are in the unhappy position of suddenly finding ourselves with a post-16 structure which will not match demand and developments. Since many schools already have small sixth forms and since the numbers in this age range will fall sharply in the 1980s there may well be seats to spare in the schools while the colleges of FE, some already flooded out, may not be able to take all the young people who apply to them.

The second major problem in FE was also a little black cloud, no bigger than a man's hand, a couple of years ago. I refer, of course, to the activities of the Training Services Agency. The TSA, as its name implies, is concerned with training and not with education, though one recognises that these are complementary aspects of a single process. In the previous chapter, I mentioned the unfortunate division between education and training which has bedevilled technical education and still does. Now we have a situation where the TSA, charged with the responsibility for the country's training effort, has to rely upon FE as the major national provider of education and training. There is an obvious risk that this division could become even more marked.

There is an urgent need at the moment, not only to unify the educational provision for the 16 to 19s, but to unify our arrangements for training and education. Unlike the FE interests, the TSA has a policy and it speaks with a single voice. Because of the way it is funded, the TSA can adopt direct and single-minded approaches to the problems about young people and employment that badly need tackling. If you detect a faint note of admiration here, you are right. Inside the colleges of FE there is admiration for TSA initiatives, concern at its muscle-flexing, jealousy of its resources, suspicion of its motives, and concern at its naïveties. Let us hope that the possibilities for friction inherent in this uneasy partnership will not materialise.

The third problem is less tangible but no less real. The appearance of the TSA courses comes at a time when our time-honoured pattern of apprenticeship, of training, and technical education is breaking-up. Very soon, under the impact of TEC and BEC, national certificate schemes will disappear and there will be a wholly new and baffling structure of technician education. And it is probable that its arguable benefits will be extended downwards to craft training in due course. At the same time our traditional method of day-release is also losing favour and becoming outmoded. Already in the engineering and construction industries first-year training is carried out on a full-time basis, though the much-vaunted modular system has not yet made any significant impression.

In fact, we are seeing a significant swing towards full-time and block-release vocational education and we have to come to terms with it. In several countries on the Continent, craft and technician education has traditionally been carried out on a full-time basis and our practices, as members of the EEC, are likely to be much influenced by the European experience. This is no bad thing. We are far too parochial in our educational thinking (apart from a deplorable habit of seizing upon outmoded American ideas and practices) and we must learn to look beyond the grey and misty waters of the Channel, no matter how eccentric or immoral the natives on the mainland may strike us.

So although there are several issues which may remain unresolved for some time (given our national *penchant* for tinkering with the ramshackle rather than rebuilding on a greenfield site) FE colleges can look forward to the 1980s and the future with considerable confidence.

We have a full order book. More and more well-motivated young people will continue to turn to FE for full-time general education and our vocational courses will continue to grow in variety and popularity. Our utility and versatility have at last been recognised and we are beginning to bask in the glow of public esteem—which is a pleasant experience after years in the wilderness. Adult education, resilient as ever, will no doubt rise Phoenix-like from the ashes of the Russell Report, and the rapid development of our other community activities will be limited only by deficiencies in accommodation and staffing.

So the glass is set fair. I hear the strains of 'A calm sea and a prosperous voyage'. Let us go below and be snug together and drink to the further success of Further Education. Even if the winds of change should beat upon us, we are tolerably well-furnished and provided, though our decks are somewhat overcrowded with pilgrims. But our course is clearly charted and we sail with confidence out into the morning and over the rim of the world.

Glossary of terms used in further education

Academic board

A representative body of the full-time teaching staff normally responsible to the governing body for the planning, coordination, development, and oversight of the academic work of the college.

Apprentice

A young worker between the ages of 16 and 21 employed under indentures or agreement in a skilled trade. Often called a craft apprentice. Apprentices in engineering and building form the bulk of day-release students in technical colleges.

Art (college or school of)

Courses in fine art and design are mainly provided in colleges or schools of art and also in art departments of some technical colleges.

BEC

Business Education Council. Established in 1974 to establish, promote and maintain a set of awards having a national and international currency, to devise and approve courses leading to its awards, and to promote advances in business education at sub-degree level.

Block release

A system under which employers send students (with pay) to colleges for periods of full-time study, ranging from two to eighteen weeks per session.

Business studies

The term used to describe courses, particularly for national certificates and diplomas and degrees, which are intended for those aiming at careers in business and in office employment.

Chartered Engineer (C Eng)

Corporate member of one of the professional engineering bodies that form the Council of Engineering Institutions.

City and Guilds

The City and Guilds of London Institute is the largest of the examining bodies in technical education. It prepares syllabuses, holds examinations, and awards qualifications, for craftsmen, technicians and others.

CNAA (Council for National Academic Awards)

An autonomous body set up in 1964 to award degrees, comparable in standard with awards granted and conferred by universities, on students in non-university establishments.

College of higher education

The name being given to some 'diversified' colleges of education and to some new institutions created by combining colleges of education with FE institutions.

Craft courses

Courses, usually day-release, for young men who intend to become craftsmen in engineering, building, etc.

Craftsman

A worker in industry performing skilled practical tasks.

Certificate of Secondary Education (CSE)

Examination instituted in 1963, administered by fourteen regional boards, designed for pupils of average ability who have taken a five-year secondary school course.

Day-release

The system by which employers allow employees to attend college without loss of pay for one day per week for further education. Most of these students are apprentices or trainees and the courses are known as day-release or part-time day courses.

DES

Department of Education and Science—formerly the Ministry of Education.

Diploma of Higher Education (Dip HE)

A two-year course, with two A level entry, offered by colleges of higher education, polytechnics and FE colleges.

General Certificate of Education (GCE)

Our major national external examination instituted in 1951, administered by eight examining boards. There is the ordinary level (O level) examination at 16-plus and the advanced level (A level) at 18-plus.

HMI

A member of Her Majesty's Inspectorate.

Higher National Certificate (HNC)

Nationally recognised qualification gained after two years' part-time study in various fields, including building, engineering, science and business studies. Regarded as high-level technician qualification.

Higher National Diploma (HND)

Qualification approaching the standard of a degree gained after a two-year full-time or three-year sandwich course.

Junior college

An institution providing education, both full-time and part-time, for young people over 16.

LEA (local education authority)

Charged with the duty of providing education in accordance with the 1944 Education Act and with the policy of the DES.

National Union of Students (NUS)

Provides vacation work, travel, insurance and advice on student grants for its 770,000 members in universities, colleges of FE, and colleges of education. Acts as a pressure group in higher and further education.

Operative

Worker who, using machinery or plant, carries out specific operations that do not need traditional 'craft' skills.

Ordinary National Certificate (ONC)

The nationally recognised qualification in engineering, business studies, construction and sciences obtained after a part-time course of two years. It approximates to A level and is recognised, depending on the level of pass, as an entrance qualification for some universities, for CNAA degrees, college diplomas and for HNDs.

Ordinary National Diploma (OND)

As the *ONC*, but gained by full-time study which allows a broader and deeper treatment of the curriculum.

Polytechnic

Large institution offering full- and part-time courses at degree and sub-degree level in a wide range of disciplines.

Regional examining bodies

Six independent regional organisations providing examinations, mainly non-advanced, in technical, commercial and general subjects, etc.

Sandwich courses

Courses consisting of alternate periods of not less than eighteen weeks of full-time study in a technical college and of supervised experience in industry, usually extending over several years. Students can be either college-based or works-based, i.e. sponsored by the firms in which they spend their industrial training period.

TEC

Technician Education Council. Established in 1973 for the development of policies for schemes of technician education for persons at all levels of technician occupation in industry and elsewhere.

Technician

The term 'technician' is applied to a wide range of responsible jobs involving a higher level of scientific and technical knowledge than that needed by a craftsman but below that needed by a technologist.

Technician courses

Part-time courses intended to qualify students for technicians' posts in various fields of industry.

Technician engineer

Non-chartered engineer, holding responsible position in engineering, expert in the application of specific engineering techniques.

Technologist

The technologist has degree level qualifications (usually in science, mathematics or engineering) and is engaged in applying his knowledge to technological problems.

Tertiary college

An institution providing education, both full- and part-time, for young people over 16.

TSA

Training Services Agency. One of the two executive branches of the Manpower Services Commission set up in 1974, responsible for the promotion of training for employment. Controls the Industrial Training Boards (ITBs).

Printed in England for Her Majesty's Stationery Office by The White Rose Press, Mexborough and London.   Dd 497087 K56 10/76